A SCIENTIFIC SEARCH FOR HAPPINESS AND CONTENTMENT

The Universal Life Force

By
Dr. Michael F. Whitaker

Copyright 2018 Dr. Michael F. Whitaker
A Scientific Search for Happiness and Contentment: The Universal Life Force:
All rights reserved. No part of this book may be reproduced or utilised in any form or by any means, electronic or mechanical, including photocopying, recording or by any information storage or retrieval system, without permission in writing from the publisher, except in the case of brief quotations embodied in critical reviews and certain other non-commercial uses permitted by law. Inquiries should be addressed to the Permissions Department via tomwhitakerbooks@gmail.com.
ISBN: 9781791752422

www.universallifeforce.webs.com

DEDICATION

I would like to dedicate this book to my children, Benjamin, Thomas and Rachel, their children and to those who follow, in the hope that the wisdom required to live in a benign and harmonious co-existence with their fellow beings can be recognised within these pages.

A SCIENTIFIC SEARCH FOR HAPPINESS AND CONTENTMENT
The Universal Life Force

CONTENTS

FOREWORD	8
ACKNOWLEDGEMENTS	10
1. INTRODUCTION Asking Big Questions	11
2. I WANT TO BE HAPPY Happy Moments	13
3. CHILD'S PLAY Truth, Morality and Perspective	17
4. THE TEENAGE YEARS Self-doubt, Desirability, Hormones, Changing Boundaries	20
5. WHY ARE YOU SO SELFISH? Selfishness, Selflessness, Charity, Survival Strategies	27
6. THE UNIVERSAL FORCE The Big-Bang, Sinusoidal Waves of Energy Energy Management and Conservation Tuning and Harmonic Resonance, Standing Waves Energy Vortices, Matter, Neutrinos, Electrons, Quarks Particles, Gluon, Bosons, String Theory Bonding, Nucleons, Protons, Neutrons, Electromagnetism Atoms, Gravity, Stored Energy Molecules, Larger Structures, Amino Acids The Selfish Universe, Entropy, Adjacent Universes Templates, Dark Energy, Phase Tuning, Polarity Newton's Laws of Thermodynamics	31

7. THE DEVELOPMENT OF LIFE 53
Meteorites, Water, Tetrahedrons, Carbon, Amino Acids
RNA, Viruses, Mutation
Genes, Genotypes, Chromosomes, Genome
DNA Nucleus, Outer Host Cell Communication
Evolution

8. GREY MATTER 66
Older Reptilian Brain, Limbic System, Cerebral Cortex
Abstraction, Coding, Sleep, Dreams, Concentration
Neurotransmitters, Synapses, Pain Pleasure Syndrome

9. EVOLUTION OF THE BRAIN 76
Perception, Behaviour, Feelings, Emotions, Fight-or-Flight
Pleasure Opiates, Withdrawal, Survival Equations

10. THE SURVIVAL EQUATION 89
Security Scores, Abstract Activities
Science, Humour, Art, Fiction, Music, Games

11. THE TRIPARTITE SYSTEM 103
Pre-Frontal Cortex, Neocortex, Reptilian Brain
Pain, Pleasure, Contentment

12. COOL DUDES AND WIMPS 109
Signal Strength, Strong Signal, Weak Signal
Personalities, Introverts, Extroverts, Flat Liners

13. OTHER FACTORS 124
Personality Traits, Anger, Empathy, Subconscious
Esteem-Conscience: Our Inner Policeman

14. LOVE AND ROMANCE 137
Passing On The Genetic Code, Appraising Partners, Beauty
Love, Being In Love, Jealousy, Pain Of Separation

15. SIGMUND FREUD 153
Id, Ego, Superego, Subconscious

16. DISTORTION OF THE TRIPARTITE SYSTEM   156
Mental Illness, Depression, Drugs, Alcohol, Malfunctions

17. ORIGINS OF LIFE ON EARTH   162
Environmental Change, Comets, RNA- DNA Seeding
Energy Food Chain, Parasites

18. EXTENDED FAMILY OF DNA   171
Cooperative Pyramid, Benign Competitors, Shared Benefit
Security, Community, Civilisation, Globalisation
Democracy, Market Economy, Stock Market
Space Exploration, Robots

19. A PLACE FOR GOD   175
Religion, Moral Codes, Comfort, Belief in Something More
Self-Sustaining Religious Security Pyramids
Opportunism, Appropriation, Corruption, Enforcement, Struggle
Christianity, Monotheism, Buddhism, Confucianism
Enlightenment, Sanctity of Life

20. SAVE THE WORLD   180
Understanding Human Behaviour
Security, Happiness, Contentment

21. EVOLUTION OF A SECURITY PYRAMID   183
Family, Tribes, Kingdoms, Nations, States
Democracy, Fair Trade, Tariffs, Trade Security Pyramid

22. PEACE ON EARTH   186
Global Stability, Interdependence, Multinational Business
Skills, Companies, International Agreements, Free Movement
Commercial Enterprise, Regulatory Mechanisms, Globalisation
Greed, Excess, Discontent, Revolution

23. SURVIVAL OF THE CONTENTED   191
A Controlling Force, Conservation of Energy, Delaying Entropy
Opiates, Pleasure, Happiness, Contentment, Survival Equations

REFERENCES	194
ATTRIBUTES	195
OTHER PUBLICATIONS BY THE AUTHOR	196
SYNOPSIS Our Place In The Universe, The Universal Life Force	198
ABOUT THE AUTHOR	202

FOREWORD

This story represents my philosophies and ideals, as a young man during my late teens and early twenties, and my search for an understanding of life and my place in the Universe. The philosophies were initiated more or less during the late sixties and developed further in the seventies and eighties within a domestic environment, provoked entirely by discussions between me and my elder sister. Despite recent work supporting the principles discussed and illustrated in the original manuscript, there are still many ideas discussed within this text for testing. I believe, given time, they will also prove to be correct.

My sister was a self-taught philosopher, in her early forties, following the logic and style of the classical philosophers such as Plato and Socrates. She was determined to educate her younger brother, a young student geologist, in the finer points of their rationale. Although fascinated by their philosophies, I was much more interested in presenting alternative interpretations based on my early scientific education and intuition. The battle began.

The discussions were often long, marathon-scale occasions, often extending from the early evening to the following morning, each of us determined to prove our point. Such occasions continued for several years, with an opportunity after each meeting to consider implications before battle recommenced. This pushed me rapidly into scientific and philosophical areas I would otherwise never have visited. It made me consider the widest implications of principles that seemed to extend their influence into every aspect of scientific endeavour. As a result, though not realising it at the time, I found myself constructing a whole new approach to this area of philosophy, an approach based on the rational of modern science rather than the archaic methods and beliefs of a bygone era many centuries old.

Curiously, I never took these philosophical and scientific ideas any further. For a long time, I regarded my concepts more as playful ideas, purely for private and personal consumption. A few early attempts at trying to present or discuss the concepts further with colleagues or friends were met with unfavourable, if not derisive, comment. It didn't encourage me to continue. It wasn't until 1978 when I received a phone call from a former university colleague telling me of a book he had just read called the *Selfish Gene* by Richard Dawkins that I suddenly realised that there was actually real merit to such concepts. Just hearing the title of the book told me that he had arrived at the same basic idea and that most likely everything I had been developing over the years was going to be presented within those pages. I was so convinced of this that I couldn't even bear to open the book and read those words, which I thought belonged to me. This of course, was a futile and unfair perception. If I had been more organised and confident, I could have written something similar. It was my own lack of perception to see this potential and the reality that other scientists could have also been experimenting with these ideas at the time. Nevertheless, and probably to my detriment, I still have not been brave enough to read any book by Richard Dawkins.

So why bother now when several of these concepts have now been subsequently confirmed and published by others. A good question – one I kept asking myself in the late eighties as I finally began writing the first manuscript. Well, my only excuse is that similar to all individuals who have developed ideas independently of others, they still like to feel the ideas and concepts belong a little to themselves. But it is not only that – I also feel that, because of the isolated environment in which the concepts were developed, they still have many unique insights, not grasped by the established thinkers in this particular field of scientific philosophy. My hope is that the reader will be able to gain from my own particular views and explanations and build further, with argument and discussion, their own personal and unique insight into the mysterious world of the *Universal Force,* the driver of the consequent *Life Force.*

ACKNOWLEDGEMENTS

I would like to thank my wife, Carol, for her patience during the editing and production of this book.

I would also like to thank my son, Thomas, for his considerable help in the editing of the original manuscript and its preparation for publication. Without his encouragement I suspect it would never have been completed.

1

INTRODUCTION

There comes a moment in everyone's life. You may be fifteen, sixteen or twenty-five. But the moment arrives, and when it does, you want answers. You feel there has to be a reason. At this moment nothing makes sense. Nothing in life is straightforward anymore. Parents begin to chastise you for what seem to be trivialities. They don't understand you anymore and their reactions are strained. The values you once held as normal are being challenged. All around you is injustice and inequality. Nothing seems right. The world seems to have changed and you feel lost. It is the moment you ask:

'What is the purpose of life?'

'What am I really doing here?'

Despite the very profound nature of such questions, for some it is a fleeting moment. They ask the questions and are told there is no answer. Just get on with your life and enjoy what you can – and this is what they do. Such a response is not uncommon. However, for some, there is not enough time or energy to push further, to question, because the necessities of daily life – work, family and all the rest – require more hours than there are in a day.

There are others, however, who are not satisfied with such answers and do wish to know more. They search the religious philosophies and for some they find answers there. Such philosophies offer the hope and comfort of a life everlasting, a story of the triumph of good and righteousness, of justice. It offers warmth and security for the outrageous misfortunes that may befall us, for the moments when we suffer unjustly, be it health or otherwise.

For others, they find a compromise within atheism, where they do not accept the tenuous beliefs of religious faith, of an omnipotent benefactor, and settle for the answer that we are a chemical mixture, governed by the laws of physics, within a cold chemical Universe, without purpose and direction. A fortuitous chemical combination valid for the moment, but with time, our evolving chemical mixture becomes out of balance and so can no longer be sustained. This way our life begins and ends. This is indeed a bleak and cold philosophy to a life that experiences the finest detail and beauty of its surrounding Universe, the Universe that will eventually destroy us. Surely there has to be more to it than this. How can we live our life carrying only this knowledge? How can we bring a child into this world to tell them that there is really no point to you being here? Such a question seems almost unbearable to ask. There has to be an alternative.

The story I am about to tell represents the period within the late sixties and early seventies during my late teens and early twenties which brought about a particular combination of scientific and emotional experience to bear on this most important question. During this period I found happiness; I found 'God' and the reason to be. This last sentence is not said lightly. By the time you have finished reading this short book you will see, without doubt, the full scientific explanation for all these fundamental areas of our existence. It is not to be scoffed at as hocus pocus, or some kind of religious mania, or the insane ramblings of an unbalanced mind. It is a rational, beautiful and fascinating understanding of our existence. It provides a basis to understand our behaviour, the complexities of our emotions and the way we must live to achieve a fulfilled and satisfying life. The answer is here and it isn't '42' (Douglas Adams, 1978).

2

I WANT TO BE HAPPY

My journey began with one simple question: Why is happiness so elusive? Why is it, when so many good things fall into place in our lives, and we should be feeling on top of the world, a sense of gloom can descend upon us? Why is it after the initial elation from a turn of good fortune, by the end of the day we can return to the same old glum outlook we had previously? It seems we can never sustain happiness for very long (Figure 1).

Figure 1

Similarly, although we often don't like to admit it, during some situations considered by most to be sad, we can feel relatively unstressed and content with ourselves and not at all upset. We may even feel obliged to strike a sombre pose out of respect because it seems more appropriate –

ridiculous really, and all quite frustrating. This roller-coaster ride we all have to endure through our life seems uncontrollable. Our emotions will have their way. We simply cannot wrap happiness up in a little bag or pop it into a jar for later use. Riches matter not. No matter how many Porsches sit in the drive, no amount of money will guarantee the next day will be happy.

Why should this be? Is there an explanation? Can we really control it?

As always, some people accept this situation instinctively. They attribute it to their personal circumstances and environment.

'I'm far too busy.'

'So much to do.'

'Not enough money.'

'Not enough help.'

Some blame it on others, their problem spouse, their problem children, their boss at work, and others. Yet many of the wealthy and famous still have the same problems even when there seems nothing left to bother them. They pay psychiatrists handsomely and spend hours discussing why they still feel unhappy.

It seemed crucial to me that we should be able to explain and understand every aspect of our emotional state and our pursuit of happiness. We need to know why we act and feel the way we do. The knowledge and skills to manage our own psyche should be an integral part of our education. Many of our more serious social problems could be avoided if we understood this part of our behaviour better than we currently do. We rely on a chaotic and outdated series of guidelines and rules and continue to educate each new generation with the same inadequate and sometimes erroneous doctrines.

I was prompted to think in depth about such principles, especially those underlying happiness, when I was about twelve years old. At this time my parents occasionally held parties at home. Alcohol was consumed by the adults, and I was left to wander amongst them listening to their cheery noise not really understanding the effects of alcohol. Quite often in these occasions, the people in this cheery state would remark how sullen I looked and that I should cheer up. These comments, that I didn't look very happy, were further compounded by one of my teachers at school. He took me aside and asked, in a concerned tone, if I was happy and whether there were any problems at home. There weren't any problems as far as I was concerned. I was astonished that he had asked. I thought I was happy.

Such questions and comments really focused my attention. It made me look at myself for the first time. It made me look closer at the world around me. Most of all, it made me examine what was it exactly that made me happy and the principles underlying such happiness.

THE AUTHOR AGE 12 The only player without a convincing smile.

Figure 2

If happiness meant smiling, then I could certainly do that as well as anyone else. However, as everyone knows, you immediately notice that it is difficult to sustain a smile for more than a few seconds. Also, no matter how hard I tried, I could not simulate a smile or smile purposely, especially whilst being photographed.

Another problem was that I didn't seem to enjoy some of the more traditional fun activities. Fairgrounds, for example, after the age of ten, held little interest. As I grew older, parties became more stressful occasions than fun. Such occasions can be quite complex arrangements of public performance and personality competitions. Speaking with one person alone can be much more relaxing than the brawl of a group. I am speaking of personal happiness when I mention groups and parties. I do not deny the stimulation of new ideas and other benefits that such occasions can bring. I merely highlight that despite the new information and sometimes inspiration that larger groups can give, the detailed interactions that take place during such intercourse are not easy to negotiate and can leave you feeling ignored, slighted, aggrieved – in other words, unhappy.

At this young age, if I was to describe what sort of situations made me happy, the emphasis would be on 'moments' rather than 'sustained periods'. Such moments could include singular periods during the reading of a book, a particular part of a song or piece of music, the acquaintance of a pretty young girl, walks in the countryside, scoring a goal at football, the anticipation of Christmas day, among others. There could be many of these moments within a day, but somehow these moments rather than any others brought joy. So what exactly controls these moments? What decided these moments rather than any other moment would make me smile and why? What was the purpose of these moments, and why were they necessary considering most of the day was spent quite successfully without smiling?

During the late sixties, whilst I was in my teens, I began to study these questions more earnestly. This was not pure accident. It is a time when we all become more aware and more conscious of ourselves and our surroundings. Most of my friends and classmates were actively engaged in such discussions. I rarely took part, however, as their ideas were often crude and bizarre. Instead, I started my own simple investigation of when and where I could say I was happy, both present and past, and to note the circumstances surrounding those moments.

3

CHILD'S PLAY

Following the rules can bring times of contentment

I began with my recollections of early childhood, a period I seemed to recall as being reasonably happy. Childhood is often believed to be one of the happiest times in our lives, a not-too-surprising conclusion considering the great care that most parents take at this time to provide shelter and protection. Inside this contained environment, a child is free from the pressures of the outside world. Parents provide security, sustenance and care and keep you out of danger (Figure 3).

Figure 3

A photograph in Figure 4 shows a young child in a playpen happily playing with his toys. In this orderly stable setting, the child can develop a normal and balanced understanding of this small world around him. The only condition imposed onto this world is that the child stays within the playpen.

Figure 4.

Philosophically, the child has learnt his first 'truth', that if he behaves and follows the simple rule to stay within the playpen, then life remains happy. But if he tries to get out, then he can be subject to the discomfort of being firmly returned inside. He has also learnt his first moral code of behaviour, and if he follows this code and abides by the rules, then there are more chances of him being happy. Figure 5 represents this understanding as a morality and perspective box. It has a defined shape and edges covering areas of behaviour considered in this child's mind as good and correct.

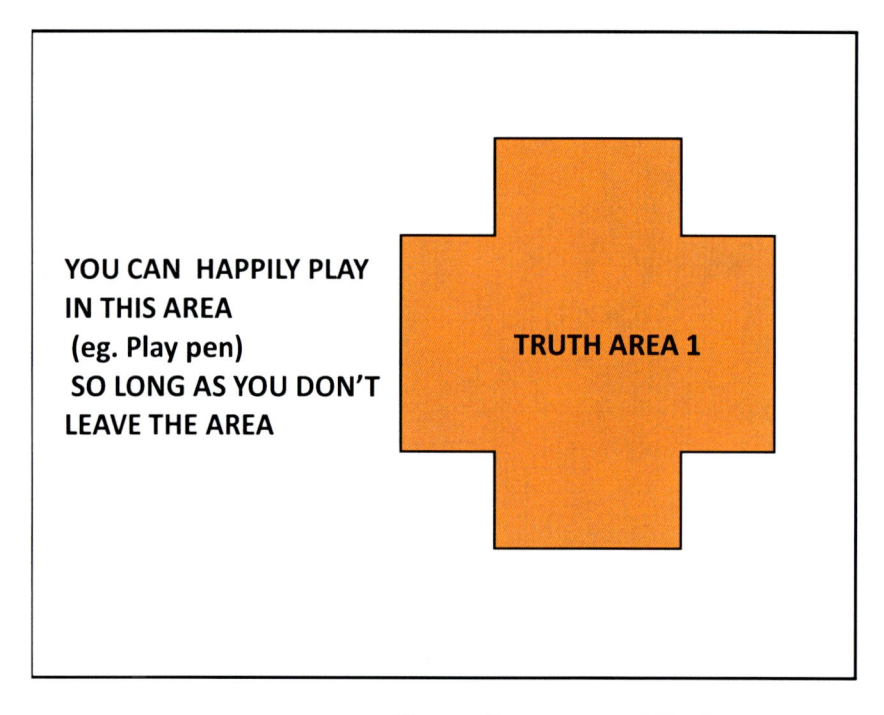

YOU CAN HAPPILY PLAY IN THIS AREA
(eg. Play pen)
SO LONG AS YOU DON'T LEAVE THE AREA

TRUTH AREA 1

Figure 5.

Now, as the child grows, he will visit a friend's house and discover whole new areas of having fun. He's allowed to indulge in a little pillow fighting in a friend's home. This wasn't true in his home, but he's not allowed to watch the television here, which he could do at home. He discovers that his friend's morality box has a different shape and doesn't entirely overlap with his as shown in Figure 6.

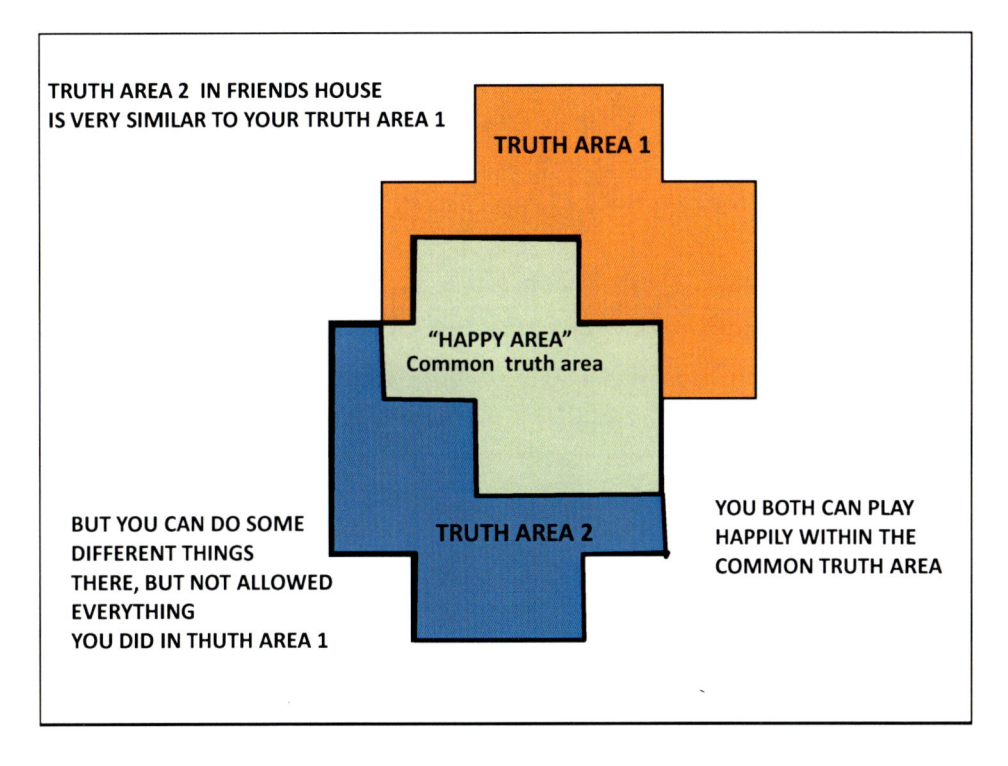

Figure 6.

So what was true in his home is not exactly true in someone else's. Philosophically it seems we quickly appreciate that 'truth' is not fixed and that it varies according to circumstances. Similarly, 'moral codes' vary. Thus, if we are to be happy, it's important that we know the rules, what is true and what is the expected moral code of behaviour. But if both the 'truth' and the 'moral code' vary, our ability to be happy is compromised. As we continue to grow, we gradually become more aware of this and attempt by trial and error to make compromises for the sake of, for example, sustaining a friendship. Generally, we can thus assume that our early childhood and schooldays are easier and can be negotiated without too much stress from the consequences, leaving many of us with memories of relatively happy days.

4

THE TEENAGE YEARS

In our teens, however, this relatively easy ride comes to an end. The hormones arrive and begin their work, changing us from carefree children into insecure, self-doubting and painfully self-conscious adults. Without these very demanding chemicals, such as testosterone and oestrogen, we were blissfully free of our need to find a mate, settle down and reproduce. Now we find ourselves with this uncontrollable urge to find a mate. Not only that, but the need to be attractive becomes paramount as well. We all want to be witty, intelligent and beautiful. However, for many of us, with one look in the mirror, we realise that nature has apparently dealt us a severe blow. An exaggerated example of this moment is illustrated by the photograph in Figure 7.

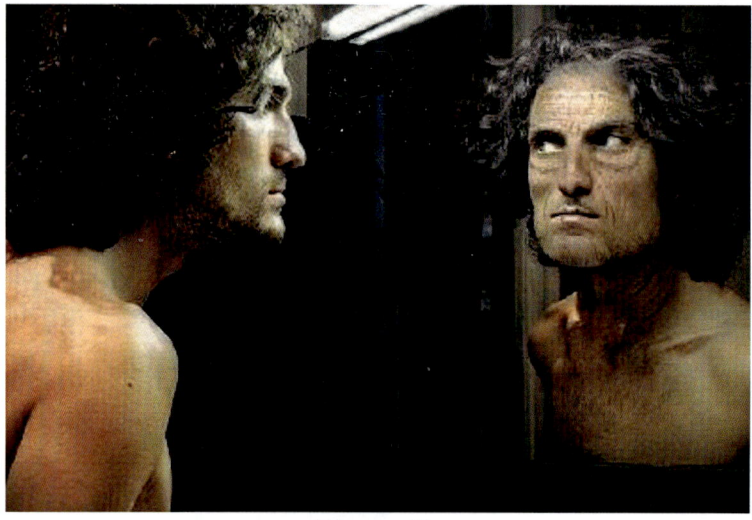

Figure 7.

As we stare disbelievingly, correcting the angle of pose and the lighting, the word 'unhappiness' takes on a whole new meaning: that nose, those ears, those teeth and, most of all, those spots. I remember thinking perhaps no one will notice, but of course, just whom did I think I was kidding?

Life could take a distinct downturn. At school, the sixth form had taken on a new social hierarchy. Sport, muscle power and brains were the previous selection criteria. Your friends and social contacts tended to be restricted to one of these groups. Those skilled at football and cricket were most revered. Those who did especially well in examinations were also admired even if they were a little aloof and – let's face it – sometimes downright odd. The muscle men were not particularly admired, but they naturally dominated. Who was I to say otherwise? At any one moment they could decide to bully or intimidate. In their eyes they were top dog, and any social contact with these people was distinctly hazardous. You always hoped they considered you okay. If they actually said 'you're okay', what a moment of relief for you. The axe would not fall that day. However, this could only be a temporary pass of safety. Isolating yourself was, again, not a guarantee of safety. Keeping out of the way amounted to hiding, an act which in itself could attract their attention and, of course, their very special treatment.

This was the way of the world during early life in an all-boys school. Girls, ah yes, girls . . . They went to the school over there . . . I even knew somebody once who had a girlfriend. Girls did not have a special place at this time, and I was happy with that. This situation, however, with the emergence of hormones, was about to change forever.

Two of my best friends throughout my entire school life seemed to disappear overnight. Previously we had played football, gone fishing, went trainspotting, played chess and generally spent our time together. Other classmates also seemed unavailable. Their conversation and humour had changed. They had a different look in their eyes and spoke about 'getting ready to go out' and 'meeting Sarah' or 'Susan' or 'Janice'. At school, a new group was appearing. A select few, some of which had been barely noticed in the class before, were now raised to this status with a new and devastating quality, something that most of us could only sit back and stare upon with envy and awe. These chosen few were . . . 'good-looking', and unfortunately 'I wasn't'. The rest of us could only look on and watch. A few early and tentative attempts with the opposite sex more or less confirmed this new sub-status. One had to somehow just accept it. There was no warning this was coming – no announcement, no negotiation or discussion. It just happened.

The sudden nature of this event relates primarily to boys. Girls awaken earlier. The mirror has been their constant companion from the age of three. They also receive their input of hormones earlier – no doubt a frustrating circumstance since at this time their potential partners are still trainspotting. I still retain a vivid memory of such a circumstance. I was eleven years old at the time and enjoyed spending time with both girls and boys. Football, nevertheless, was still my primary occupation. It happened, however, that one bright and sunny day I was following along with the 'gang', a mixed company of boys and girls along a country path towards our regular spot by a cluster of trees. This was an area where we would all usually sit and gossip. The sky was a rich deep blue and the sun always shone, of course. On the way, one of the girls stopped me, took me to one side and whispered secretively 'I'd like to see you in the bath'. I was totally bemused by this. She waited for a response. There was none. I couldn't comprehend the concept. Why should anyone be interested in watching me in the bath. A few years later it dawned on me.

This same incident also touches on the instincts I had towards morality at that age, of what was right and what was wrong, of good and bad. At that time the whole request – to see me in the bath – was 'bad' and 'wrong'. I was under the impression that for boys to see girls without clothes on was a definite 'no no' instilled into me by an amorphous rain of parental innuendo and playground anecdotes, as well as a severe dose of religious doctrine. 'Thou shalt not' was firmly imprinted into my brain, ringing out its loud and clear message, usually every time I wanted to do something, shall we say, interesting, although I can't recollect ever reading anywhere specifically 'Thou shalt not look at girls without any clothes on'. Nevertheless, this ominous tone was sufficient, even without the interference of hormones, to keep me on the straight and narrow, that is, the straight and narrow path towards our usual meeting place. A meeting then took place without further incident and without the confusions of guilt that would have inevitably consumed me should I have done otherwise. The idea felt good; the result would have felt bad. As far as I was concerned, such an alternative was immoral. It was easy then to make what I believed to be the 'right' decisions. The moral code as it stood before me then seemed to have clearer guidelines. This was another reason perhaps why many of us can recall our childhood as a happier time.

Good and bad could more easily be identified. At home, 'good' was what your parents allowed you to do. 'Bad' was anything that resulted in a clip around the ear area. The boundaries could be determined fairly accurately by careful observation of parental reaction. Washing the car (properly, that is), followed by an offer to mow the lawn (without damaging the rotary blades and tidying up the loose grass cuttings afterwards), was clearly in the 'good' area. Picking up a set of my father's old – or so I thought – wireless valves and then lobbing them one by one against the wall during a make-believe World War II grenade attack was definitely in the area of 'bad'. The sound of the minor explosion as they popped against the wall was very entertaining. The sight of my father angrily chasing me around the garden and then attempting to grab my leg as I frantically made my escape over the high garden wall was a scene that could have been taken straight out of any comic book.

Such boundaries could be, and had to be modified, outside the parental home. As already discussed, the boundaries could completely change. A strange situation exists in this world. Morality could vary from place to place. What's good in one place is bad in another. Which was right and which was wrong? The strict code of conduct or the more liberal but closely monitored carefree approach? Which code of conduct was morally correct? In such a seemingly innocent example, the answer does not seem that important. It does, however, illustrate the basis for the ambiguity inherent in the concept of morality and the anguish it can eventually cause when the circumstances become more complex. Our happiness depends on this. Throughout our lives, maintaining a steady course between these boundaries allows us pleasure or causes us pain. So if the rules are not clear and everybody has a different interpretation of where the boundaries lay then life could get a bit tricky, perhaps even become a nightmare as it does for some. Our morality and perspective boxes do not completely overlap, and as we meet a wider and greater variety of people, all with differently shaped morality boxes, then it is obvious we have to tread very carefully as we travel on through this life. Being brought up in a liberal environment, perhaps even a chaotic and unstable environment, where the rules are so vague or even changed every other day, one must find it hard to suddenly find yourself squeezed by the bottlenecks of more rigid regimes. You may feel morally correct, yet you're being punished. 'Such is life,' you might say, leaning on years of further experience. But it does seem unnecessary.

For the time being, I'll leave this point here and take it up later as we progress. However, just before we do leave it entirely, I would like to consider the word 'truth' again. If something is true, then it has to be right, and should it not be true, then it has to be wrong. Then it is also true to say that one of the above moralities is right and the other wrong, suggesting an underlying all-pervasive 'truth'. It is a term used by poets, statesmen and philosophers alike, not to mention politicians. They always tell the truth. It is an important word, a noble word to be carried like a banner before us.

Strangely, as a child it seemed difficult to tell the truth. It was very easy to lie. Amongst our own friends everybody seemed to lie. They told outrageous stories about themselves and their exploits without blinking an eyelid. Nobody seemed to care or worry. It was almost a form of entertainment.

'My dad grabbed a robber yesterday and threw him into prison.'

'Yeah, well, last week my dad found an escaped tiger in our garden and had to fight with it before the circus men came.'

It was also commonplace for children to say that you had found something when in fact they had taken it, usually not directly stealing it but acquiring it by very dubious means. With the help of a little parental guidance and the growing awareness of our peers, we would slowly aspire to a better understanding of what we believed to be truth and morality. It would allow us to feel more at peace and one with ourselves and others. As we grew a little older, these values would remain the cornerstones of our existence. How we perceived them and responded to them would shape our personality, our ability to be positive, to be cheerful and, of course, happy. But with the arrival of hormones during the middle teen years came new challenges affecting each and every one of us, new challenges that could completely reshape and distort our values – the need to find a mate.

On the surface it sounds simple enough – like a game, really. Game maybe, but somehow this game seemed for real. The stakes were high. The hormones made you feel and behave differently. There was a new purpose and drive within. It had almost a sense of urgency about it. It was now 'game on'. The internal drive compelled you to look in the mirror once again. The dice was loaded. You had thrown a two, because what you saw was not a pretty sight.

We all, deep down, knew this obsession with looks was hollow. What's so special about a pretty face? Beauty is only skin-deep anyway. It's the person inside that is important. There were many seemingly wise phrases around that appeared to challenge the value of being good-looking. Personality, for example – what about an attractive personality? I could always work on that. If it wasn't quite right now I'm sure with a little work it could be made absolutely sparkling. Perhaps there was hope after all. I could develop a voice like James Mason, the strong silent approach like Clint Eastwood whilst maintaining a cool but dashing edge like James Bond. Maybe I'd just go for the Bruce Willis guts and sweat instead. Such thoughts seem comical now, but who can honestly say at this age, after seeing Sean Connery so devastatingly impress the girls, that they didn't swagger from the hips that little more as they walked home from the cinema. Even if you had the ability to pull off all this, in your mid- to late teens, it still seemed a very poor second place to be referred to as having a 'good personality'. It had the ring of a prize raspberry. If you ever overheard 'Oh, but he does have an attractive personality', it was a cue to leave the stage. Your presence, that is, your visual presence, was no longer required. It would have been as accurate to say, 'He ain't good-looking but I suppose he'll have to do'. To be genuinely called 'good-looking' was to be king. I felt very gloomy about myself. I was unhappy. But why? Why should these seemingly trivial facial features hold such power over our happiness?

Looks were not the only problem. There were clearly other, seemingly more important, areas of concern. It was during these same formative years that many of us became aware of the imbalances in life, both for ourselves and others, and their effect. We observe the 'haves and have nots', a famous phrase coined in the sixties. We see the sick and the starving and the cruelty of oppression and war. As I entered university, the focus was heavily on the plight of these people and their suffering. There were photographs and film everywhere graphically making this point. There was to be no escaping how privileged we were. We were considered the lucky ones, the 'haves', with everything we wanted and the potentially bright future of riches ahead of us. Any of our problems seemed vain and futile in comparison, and complaining or moaning would have been considered terribly 'selfish'. Compared with the not-so-fortunate, it seemed out of the question to ever consider ourselves unhappy.

5

WHY ARE YOU SO SELFISH?

Let the battle really commence

The word 'selfishness' always got in the way of being happy. It has been an unwritten buzzword hovering over the 'haves' of the 20th-century Western world. We castigate ourselves incessantly both publicly and privately with this concept of ourselves. Selfishness blatantly reminds us of the religious doctrines that we were brought up to believe. It deplores our desires and shouts at the materialistic world we have built around us. It interfered with any feeling of contentment.

My elder sister, Sheila, in her brave attempts to mould my personality into something worthwhile, would use this word liberally to describe my approach to life. She was much older than me and was over nineteen when I was born, no doubt, as an unwelcome intrusion into her late teenage world. What an inconvenience that must have been in those days. Because of the age difference, she always appeared to me like a second mum than a sister, so I was obliged to listen to her. Above all, she had a strong personality, able to hold her own in any walk of life or society occasion. Despite my untimely arrival, by the time I was old enough to notice, I remembered her as being a caring, supportive person. She also had a way of making me look up to others. Certain of her acquaintances and friends were painted as heroes, masters of their discipline and captains of the world. This was a world with challenge and adventure. She was thrilled I had decided to study geology at university. It fulfilled part of this image she tried to create. Geologists were adventurers, travelling the world in search of precious metals and oil. They could be seen trekking across a desert alone with only a map, compass and a few meagre supplies or flown in a helicopter across a wild and inhospitable wasteland. I loved it. It filled my head with wonderful pictures that inspired me to go on that bit further. I wanted to be that adventurer she painted. She willed me on through school and into university. Most of all, it was her encouragement

I turned to and looked for. She had an ability to inspire and then drive you on. However, when I turned eighteen, her attitude toward me changed. The repeated use of the word 'selfish' for my activities genuinely hurt and again made me sensitive to the idea I was rapidly being annexed to yet another unworthy sub-class in life. No matter what I did or said, it seemed my sister would deem it 'selfish'. In a way she was correct but I didn't really know why. I took it for granted that being older she was probably wiser and therefore correct.

It was during a coffee break early in my university life that a discussion first evolved around the concept of the word 'selfish'. As I sat at a table, Martin, a college friend, placed two coffees down and pushed a half-filled cup towards me. He had an exceptionally engaging sense of humour and outgoing personality which usually placed him centre stage wherever he went. He sat down looking straight at me with a mocking grin across his face as I stared accusingly at his full cup of coffee. He awaited a response.

'A selfish pig you are, Martin,' I said, trying not to smile.

'I know,' he said proudly.

'I don't know how that fiancée of yours puts up with you,' I suggested.

'She knows,' he said again proudly.

'I bet she does,' I said wryly.

'Of course she does. Everything I do is selfish,' he confirmed, emphasising the words 'everything' and 'selfish'. The way he emphasised these words was clearly intended. They rang loudly in my head. The thought that 'everything' was selfish somehow appealed. It had a sort of warped truth about it.

'What do you mean by that?' I asked, knowing that he wanted me to.

'I know everything I do is selfish,' he repeated. 'And everything you do is.'

I loved this because I knew it was true. It was music to my ears. I didn't realise at that moment all the implications; I just knew that this tiny little phrase was fundamental. It meant everything we do is selfish, not only the nasty things but also the most charitable.

This was a real 'eye-opening' moment for me. It projected my thoughts forward into a whole new territory of science and sociology I'd never entered before. With this understanding of selfishness, I could explore all kinds of new relationships and I couldn't wait to get started. Suddenly the world around me started to make a little more sense. For the first time I could begin to comprehend how my own internal feelings related to this world and the people in it.

The first conclusion arrived very rapidly. This unique interpretation of selfishness had to be linked with the Darwinian concepts of survival and the 'survival of the fittest'. In other words, everything we do is for our own survival, and so it is inevitable that everything we do would be for our purely selfish needs. It's selfish when we eat and drink because we're doing this purely to enable us to survive. Even giving away money could be regarded as a selfish act since in some way, giving that money will help you, because our survival is not just about internal bodily functions but also the external environment. It can be hostile and threatening and so very often we do things to make that environment safer. In the broadest terms, hoarding all the money and keeping it to yourself only makes others feel poorer. This makes them discontented and a possible threat to you. Therefore, giving is an insurance policy, a survival strategy. Just take the French Revolution as an example of what can happen if you don't give.

A more sensitive and emotive example can be illustrated as follows. Imagine the plight of a mother whose child is drowning in choppy cold waters. The need to save the child is paramount. Nothing else is more important. She is prepared to jump into this ferocious sea and risk her life to secure the safety of her child. In fact, she is even prepared to sacrifice her own life, if necessary, if she thought it would save the child.

Now an outside observer would consider her actions heroic and completely unselfish because she intended all the actions without any regard for herself and her own safety. Curiously this same observer might privately consider her actions entirely normal and, in some ways, expected within these circumstances. In fact, I could take this interpretation a little further and suggest that her actions might have been entirely selfish and for two specific reasons.

The first reason is entirely consistent with our original concept of selfishness. In fact, I believe that perhaps she is prepared to sacrifice herself because she could not live with the thought of allowing her child to drown. The guilt afterwards would have been too painful to live with. She would have been guilty of not trying. This guilt would have been compounded by the years of 'love' she had shared with her child being the mother and the thought of losing this child. It might have been the knowledge of the unbearable pain to come and the selfish desire to avoid this pain that prompts these apparently unselfish and heroic actions. In addition, there is a second reason which provides the fundamental mechanism driving this selfishness and, in fact, the whole purpose of survival.

The answer will take us away from the more superficial observations of human behaviour. I needed to consider more carefully how the Universe began and how the Earth was formed. I needed to know more about the very earliest development of life and its actual origins. It is a journey that would take me into the more technical world of physics, chemistry and biology. All these factors I suspected played a role in the development of the human condition, directly influencing our evolution, the way we behave and how we feel, and similarly, why the mother behaved as she did. It would take some time for me to unravel.

In the following sections, the level of detail will increase, but I hope you will appreciate it is necessary to fully understand the human condition. Most of the scientific ideas and concepts that follow resulted from several years of intense discussion and argument with my elder sister which often extended through the nights and into the following days. She was horrified by my ideas and tried her utmost to dismiss every supporting scientific concept I put forward. Despite this, I am grateful for the resistance she showed for it was at the height of these arguments that many of my scientific ideas, discussed in this book, were created.

6

THE UNIVERSAL FORCE

The origin of selfishness

At this time, in the late sixties, for academics it was normal practice to remain within your specific academic discipline and not go rooting around in someone else's laboratory. In other words, a geologist looked at rocks, sociologists looked at human behaviour, physicists studied heat and electricity and, as a consequence, few of them ever communicated or really knew what the other was doing. To some degree, I accepted this arrangement and, for the most part, did little to try and change the situation. I believed that this was how it was done and thus followed the tradition. However, this all changed for me when I discovered 'particle physics'. This was a new and exciting area of science for many and I couldn't get enough of it. I found myself reading all the journals I could find and even attended physics lectures without permission, a circumstance almost unheard of within young first- and second-year students. It was a time when all the basic particles were being discovered and words such as 'bubble chambers' and the 'Cern and Fermi Laboratories' became a part of my vocabulary. As a consequence, I became alerted to interrelationships within chemistry, physics, geology and biology that I would otherwise not have appreciated. It was in these inter-relationships that I found mechanisms driving our selfishness and the reason why in our previous story the mother was being selfish to save her own child. The answer was already evident from the moment our Universe was created, revealed in the chemical and physical processes already active since the beginning of time.

So let's go right back to that time when the Universe had only just formed. To the moment we call the Big Bang, when almost all the potential energy of the Universe was released. It is the moment when the constraining and governing powers of gravity are finally overwhelmed by the build-up of internal and repellent electrical forces.

Below is an attempt to briefly explain the more important chemical and physical processes, I believed, at that time, were involved.

The beginning of the Universe was almost certainly no small occasion. It was probably an explosion on a scale almost beyond our comprehension. Immensely powerful, and probably electromagnetic waves of energy would have been released in an instant, ripping open an energy rich void we call space. Unfortunately, since no one was there to see it, I could only guess at the complexities that may have existed at this time. Such a period must have been totally unique, a time in which the physics and chemistry of today may not have been recognisable. Nevertheless, it was still possible to employ the few available fragments of evidence to tentatively deduce some of the processes likely to have been influential and to recreate some of the events that might have followed (see Figure 8).

THE UNIVERSE

**BANG!!
Potential energy of a Black Hole shaken by the imbalance of positive-negative charges overpowering gravitational forces.**

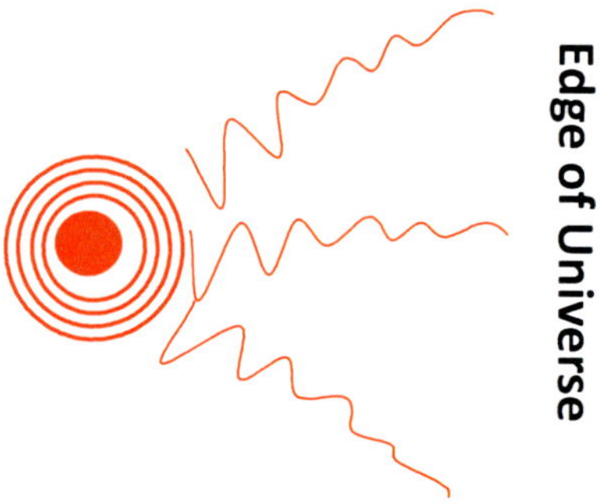

Edge of Universe

If the universe was just a big bang ......energy would simply travel and dissipate outwards at the speed of light and reduce to a flash of light within seconds.

Fortunately the Universe has a way of slowing things down and conserving energy.

It is totally obsessed with energy management and conservation.

Figure 8.

But in order to appreciate any of the complex construction processes that evolved I first had to understand more fully the nature of energy itself and the origin of 'matter' and the first particles. Having said this I am not a physicist and therefore not qualified to give the reader a full account of the classical theories and latest developments. I do not refer to Richard Feynman's famous Gauge diagrams, or Enrico Fermi's discovery of the neutron particle, or even Albert Einstein's equation E=mc2. I have, however, been able to develop my own particular understanding of the physical principles and the way our Universe behaves. Some readers may not agree with everything I suggest. However by doing this I have been able to explain some of the nuclear processes that are unclear in the existing models and for the first time understand the real reason we are here. The reality of why we exist.

To begin, within micro-seconds of the Big Bang, I envisaged an explosion of energy as electromagnetic waves expanded outwards the boundaries of space. At the same time, the explosion of energy began to 'organise itself'. This 'organisation' was important. Instead of this swirling turmoil of energy immediately dissipating to its lowest level of photons and gamma particles within a matter of moments (and literally reduced to a flash of light), the process of dissipation appears to have been significantly delayed by a series of rather special nuclear processes. In doing so, the life of the Universe was not only increased but also controlled in a manner that allowed our present and familiar cosmic architecture to evolve. Without these delaying nuclear processes the development of the Universe may have been quite different. In fact it may already have disappeared.

Firstly, where did energy come from and how can we describe it in physical terms? A question not as simple as it may sound.

At its simplest, most agree that energy is best observed as a sinusoidal curve, pulse or wave, similar to that developed by throwing a stone into a pond of water. The distance between the top and bottom of the wave basically represents the amplitude and the amount of available energy (Figure 9).

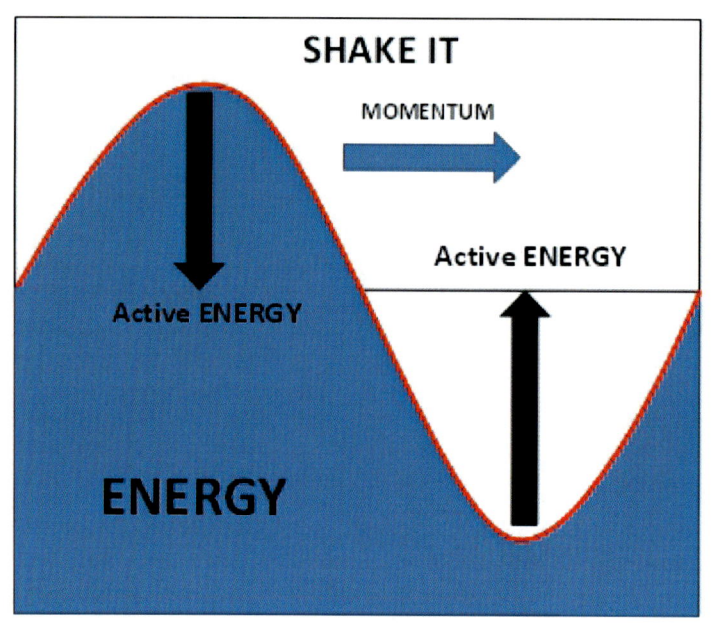

Figure 9

The frequency and momentum of this wave as it travels further increases the work this energy can do. We can actually see this energy wave travel along a piece of rope as a sinusoidal curve after we shake one end of the rope (Figure 10)

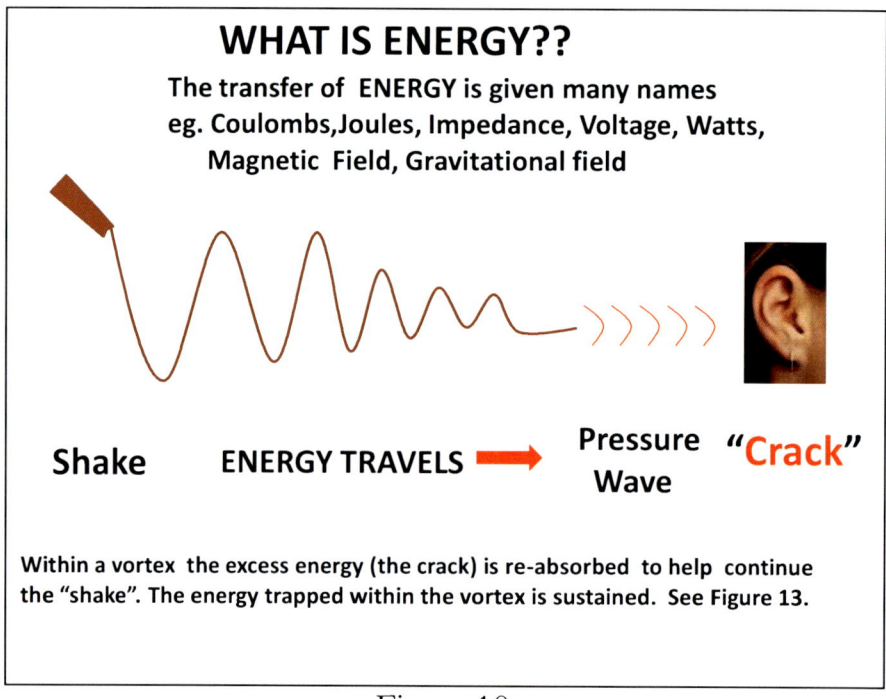

Figure 10

The resulting momentum of the wave can be observed to strike and knock objects out of the way as it travels along the rope. When it reaches the end there can be heard the familiar "crack" as the remaining energy compresses the adjacent air at the end of the rope, sending out pressure waves which we hear as a cracking sound as they vibrate our ear drum.

It's the same process for a compressed metal spring. The compressed state is analogous to a Black Hole with all its potential energy stored by the force of gravity. When the energy is greater than the force of gravity the energy expands outward as an immense wave of energy travelling within the metal spring forcing it outward. As the energy reaches the end of the spring the excess energy causes a pressure wave in the air which we hear as the familiar "boing" sound.

From my understanding of conditions prior to the Big Bang, it would appear that all the potential energy of the Universe, must have been contained within a single black hole (although I will present an alternative possibility later in this section) constrained by the forces of gravity; like the metal spring compressed and full of potential energy. But, actually, how did energy behave as it travelled away from the centre of the Big Bang and where is 'gravity' in this equation and does it control energy?

Before we delve further into the 'physics' of the Universe, it is possible some readers may not be so keen to involve themselves in the detail of this section. However, I would like to encourage the reader to continue since it is the physics of our Universe that provides the mechanisms controlling our human emotions and drives. It will explain why we came to feel emotions the way we do and, ultimately, why we feel pleasure.

Tuning and resonance
Another feature which could distort the behaviour of energy could be the effect of 'interference and resonance', as energy wavelengths come together and overlap in phase. Imagine, for example, the energy of the Big Bang to be like striking a note on the piano. If the note is struck hard, the hammer will hit the piano string causing the string to vibrate. With each vibration of the string, a pulse of energy will be transferred, via the sound board and air pressure, to our ear. The succession of sonic wavelengths associated with each vibration of the string can eventually overlap, and

reinforce, causing the energy and sound to increase or *"resonate"*. By analogy we could envisage that energy within the Universe might also resonate and that similar resonant energy maxima probably existed within the turmoil of the Big Bang. Indeed, it is not difficult to imagine, these high energy, probably electromagnetic waves, intersecting as they expand outwards like ripples in a pond.

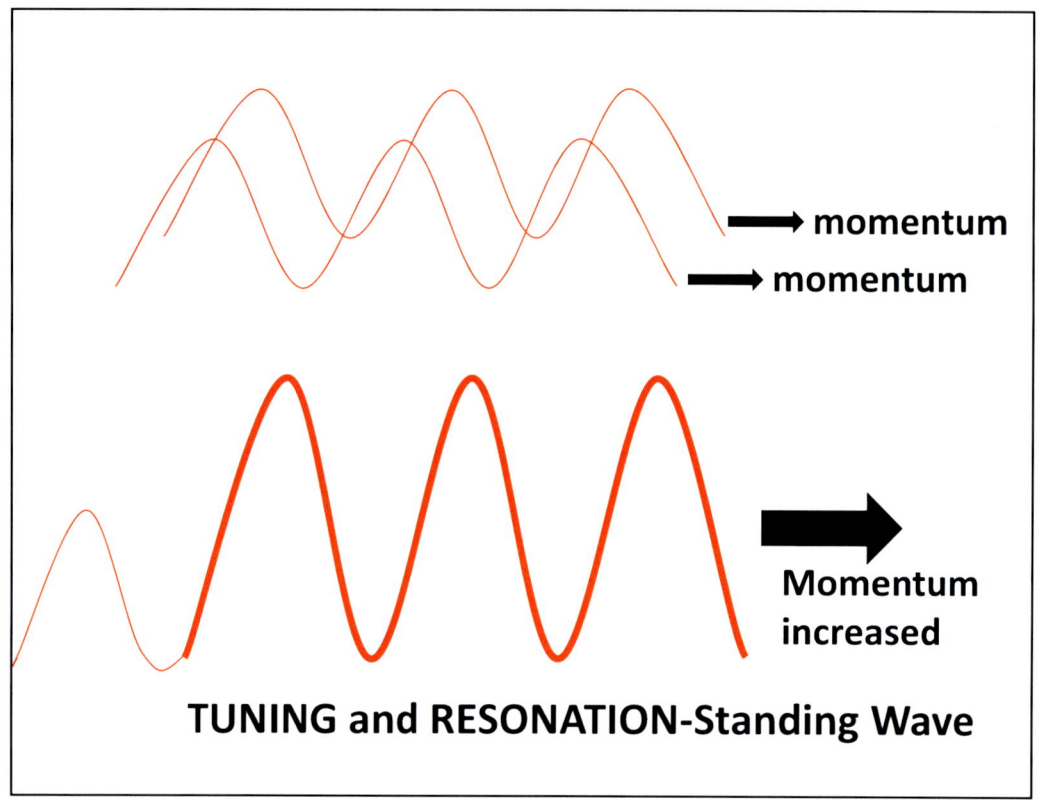

Figure 11

Such intersection points could 'tune and resonate' forming points of 'harmonic resonance,' creating 'electromagnetic standing waves' (a process sometimes referred to as 'interference wave propagation'). In effect, these standing waves would have a higher amplitude and greater momentum and so would separate to form a distinct unit of higher energy (Figure 11).

The higher energy and increased momentum would cause the direction of momentum to curve, especially when its progress forward is restricted by the surrounding lower energy ahead. This unit could eventually spin and rotate wildly to eventually form a vortex (as happens within any high-energy current). Examples of this type of motion could be observed within the bubble chambers at CERN (see Figure 12). In fact, most objects in motion tend to curve and eventually spiral. Spiralling galaxies, spiralling water eddies, spiralling air currents, tornadoes, all of these examples give inspiration to the idea that such motions are endemic to natural systems. In an electromagnetic field the current flow and direction of an electric charge can be influenced and induced to curve. All of this adds to the image of a vortex, a swirling ball of rotating spiralling energy.

Recent work by V.A.Induchoodan Menon (2010) lends some support for the above supposition. For example, he suggests confinement of the electromagnetic wave, such as a standing electromagnetic wave, not only creates mass, but also creates an electric charge. He further suggests that the mass and the spin, together with the electric charge of an electron, could be attributed to its 'standing' helical (electromagnetic) structure.

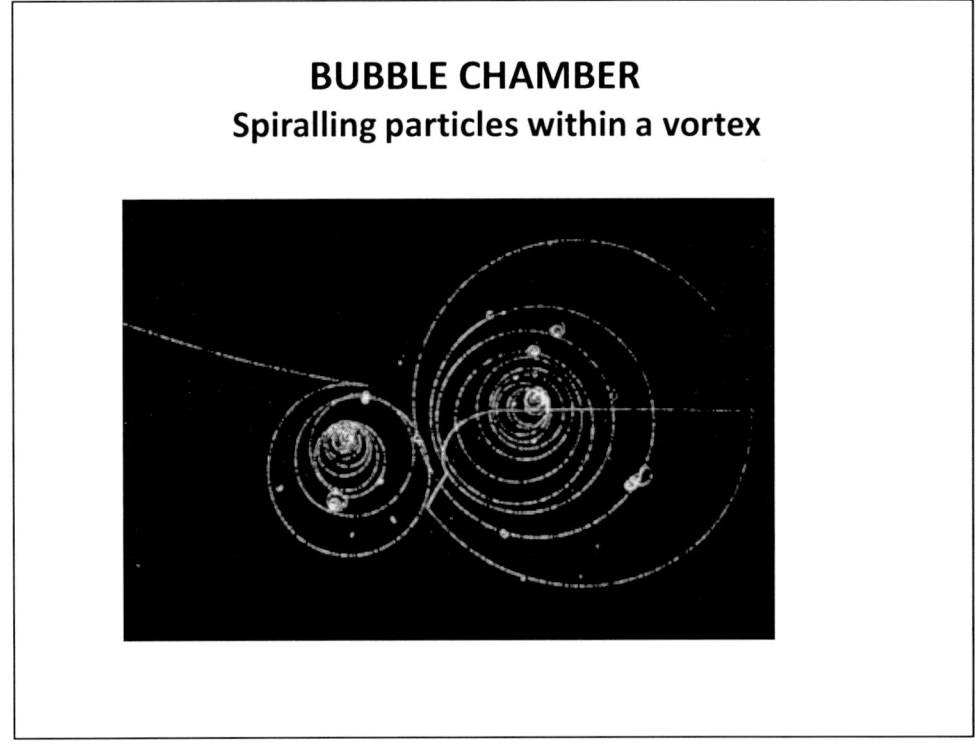

BUBBLE CHAMBER
Spiralling particles within a vortex

Figure 12

The spinning motion of the vortex could keep the energy contained and separate such that energy was never lost. Metaphorically, the excess energy at the 'tail end' of the wave would 'crack' and being contained within the vortex it would be re-absorbed, so hardly any energy is lost (Figure 13).

ORIGIN OF BASIC PARTICLES

Low energy waves — Colliding waves of energy, occasionally tune and resonate to create a Standing Wave

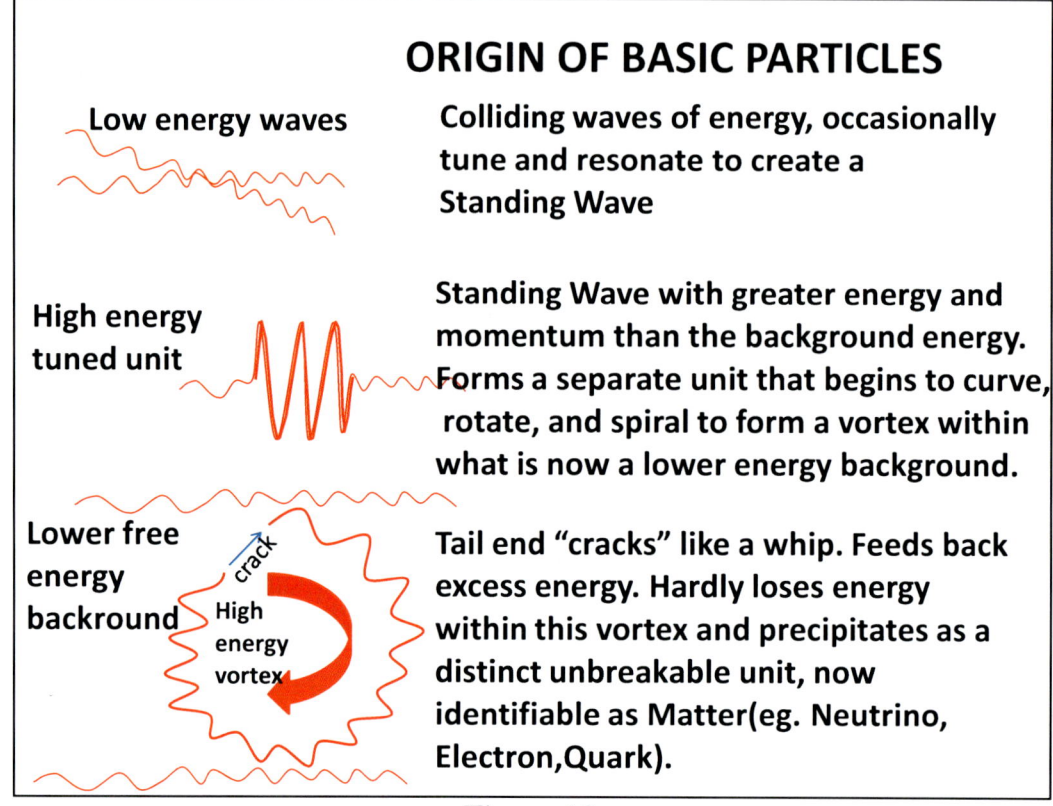

High energy tuned unit — Standing Wave with greater energy and momentum than the background energy. Forms a separate unit that begins to curve, rotate, and spiral to form a vortex within what is now a lower energy background.

Lower free energy backround — **High energy vortex** — Tail end "cracks" like a whip. Feeds back excess energy. Hardly loses energy within this vortex and precipitates as a distinct unbreakable unit, now identifiable as Matter(eg. Neutrino, Electron, Quark).

Figure 13

(The principle of the 'crack' is explained in Figures 10 and 13). This high energy unit would then separate and precipitate as 'matter' comparable to a basic particle such as a neutrino, quark or electron, a possibility also recently supported by V.A.Induchoodan Menon (2010). It is the same for all things that accelerate; they all increase in weight and momentum as the potential energy to project the object further forward increases but are restricted by their curved trajectory.

These units of swirling, spiralling energy, represented by the quarks, have a substantial amount of energy locked inside. The amount of energy represents the same amount of energy that would be used if it was allowed to travel in a straight line. If this energy was released it would suddenly hurl the object forward. The same thing happens when a training astronaut is spun around a central point, as in an astronauts training centrifuge (Figure 14).

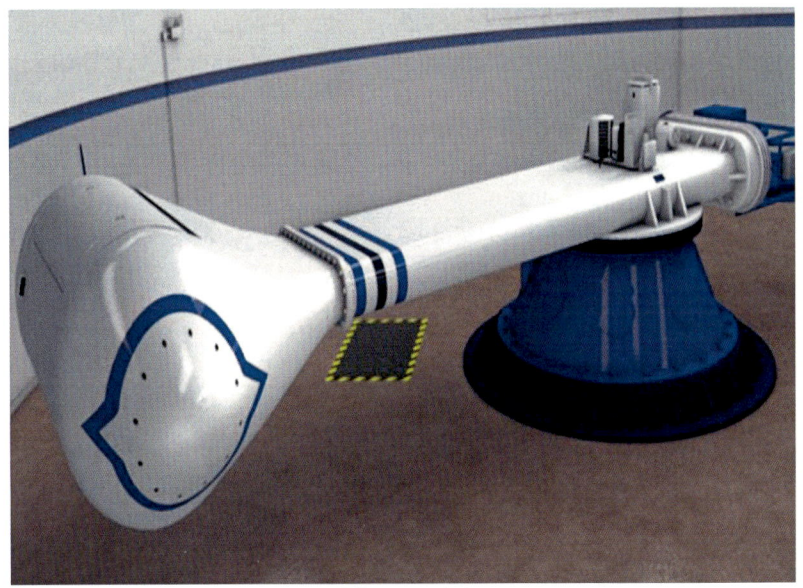

Figure 14

Because the astronaut is strapped into his seat he cannot be projected outwards across the room by the momentum provided by the increasing acceleration of the rotating centrifuge. Instead this energy is constrained inside the astronaut, building up as unreleased potential energy. As a consequence all the wave amplitudes of his body's atomic energy will increase, the force of which he will feel as extra weight (figure 15). His body will distort to accommodate this increased weight.

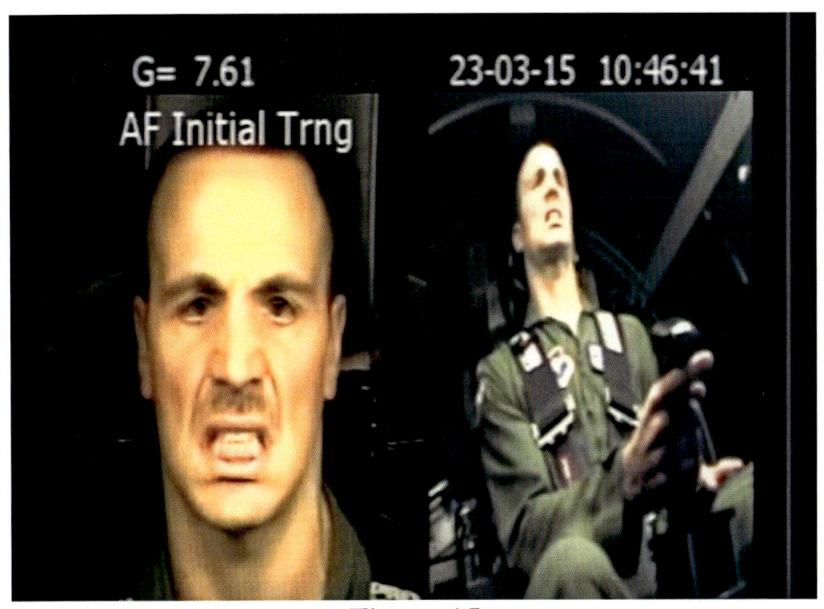

Figure 15

Quarks

In the case of our quark, the release of this energy would cause a devastating explosion. However, instead of exploding, our spiralling energy unit, (not able to go anywhere fast), vibrates violently against the immediately surrounding area of lower energy sending out vibration waves. As they travel outwards these waves eventually 'tune and resonate' as they come in phase with the other types of energy encountered in the outside energy environment. If this outside energy, perhaps includes another passing quark, their resulting vibration waves may come into phase and will probably 'resonate' with similar low-energy vibration waves from adjacent basic particles creating a binding energy unit which I believe may be equivalent to a particle called a *gluon* (Figure 16). However, current physics apparently explains the exchange of energy in interactions by the use of force carriers, called bosons.

In addition, it has recently been brought to my attention that there is an alternative String Theory, initially described by Kaluza and Klein 1921 but later developed by numerous others. Basically it also suggests there are strings of energy that vibrate. However, they believed that such structures could not be identified within our present 3 dimensional world and that it requires 4 or more dimensions to accommodate these structures. My explanation can quite easily explain similar structures within our known 3 dimensions.

In fact the process of 'tuning' and the consequent bond, created by the vibration waves emanating from the quarks, could also form the basis for a gravitational force (figure 21, p44). In other words tuning is the mechanism that creates the force we experience as **gravity**.

Current thinking appears to favour the usage of the term "Strong Force" to describe the above bonding, referring the gluon to a force carrier, as suggested many years ago, in 1963 by Eugene Wigner. Similarly a "Weak Force" is used to describe the vibration wave as radiation. However, although similar, the process and mechanism differ. In addition, the tuning and bonding mechanism described above is not regarded as a gravitational force. Nevertheless, I still prefer my own thinking since it agrees and supports the physical processes that follow and are described later in this chapter.

VIBRATION ENERGY

These high energy units vibrate violently. Their specific frequency allows tuning with other quarks as they resonate creating a gluon and so enabling a bond.

Quark — Vibration — Quark

gluon

These quarks are very stable and not exposed to external changes in the surrounding lower energy field.

PRINCIPLE OF BONDING

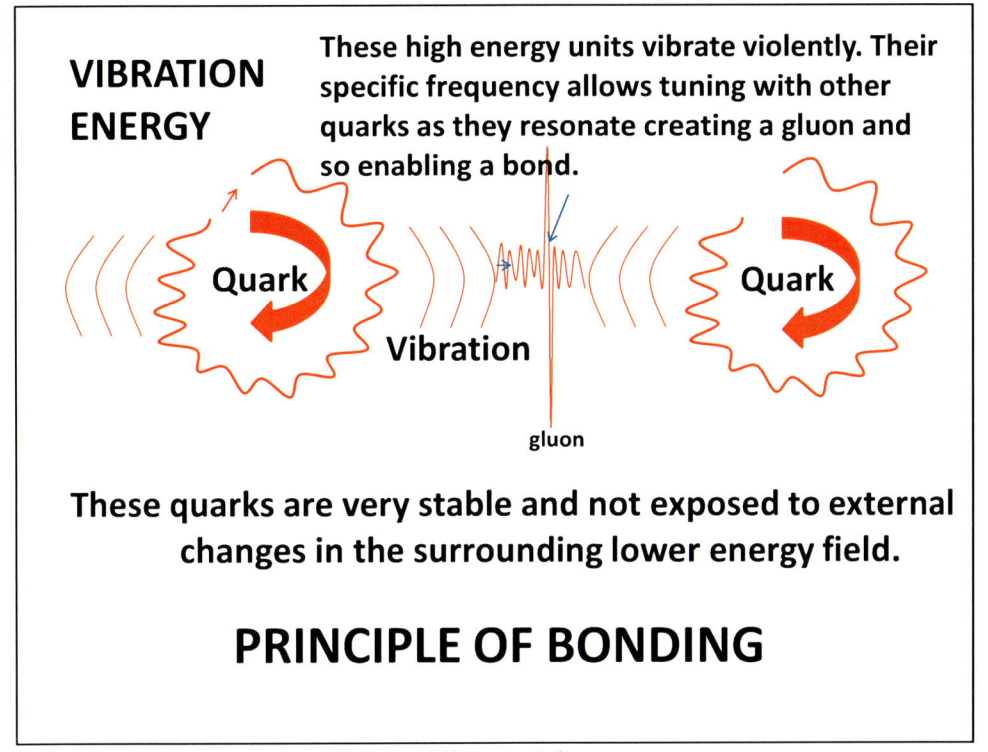

Figure 16

Nucleons (Protons and Neutrons)

Referring back to the previous section, the second quark is in effect now bonded to the first quark thus forming a larger energy particle, which I could now refer to as a proton or neutron (nucleons) (Figure 16). The resulting nucleon would probably spin and vibrate as a consequence of the swirling momentum from the internal quarks (Figure 17). Again, following the same process observed in quarks, these newly formed protons and neutrons would vibrate violently, sending out low-energy waves which could tune, bond and cluster with other protons and neutrons to form an 'atomic nucleus'. In addition, minor energy variations in the quarks within its protons and neutron would cause energy to flow within their clusters, creating polarity (see Figure 17). In effect, this flow represents the basis for **electromagnetism**.

At this stage it seems logical to believe that some of these nucleons (protons and neutrons) would become positive and so represent protons and the others negative representing neutrons. In other words, it seemed unlikely neutrons could remain neutral.

NUCLEUS OF AN ATOM (PROTONS AND NEUTRONS)

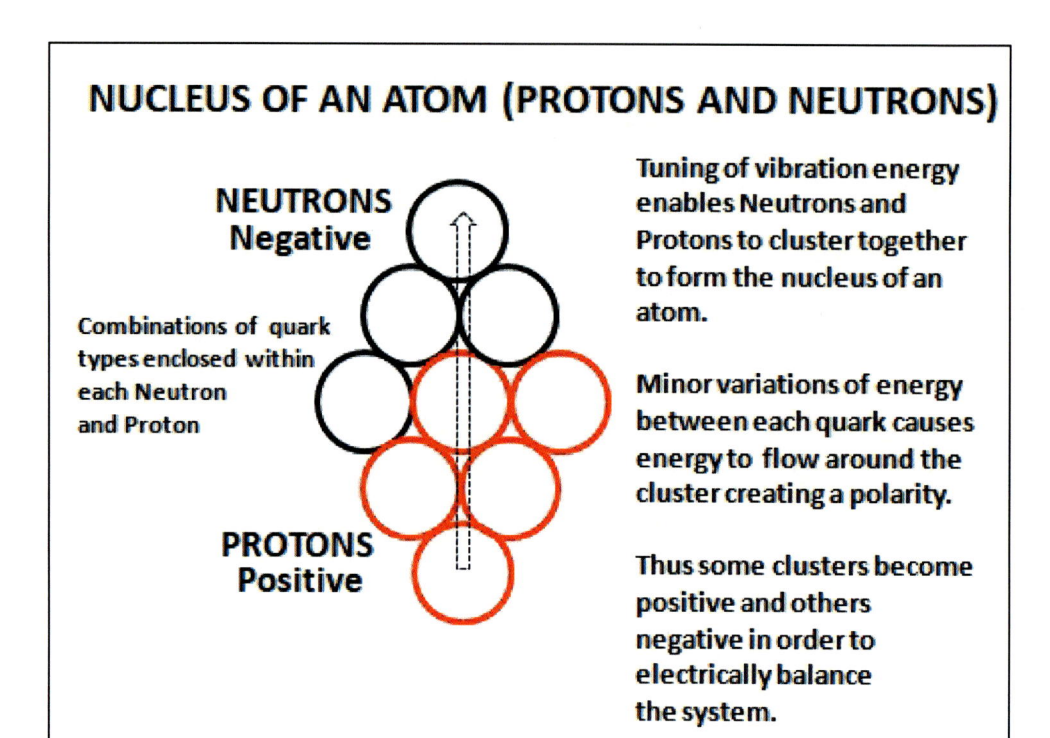

NEUTRONS Negative

Combinations of quark types enclosed within each Neutron and Proton

PROTONS Positive

Tuning of vibration energy enables Neutrons and Protons to cluster together to form the nucleus of an atom.

Minor variations of energy between each quark causes energy to flow around the cluster creating a polarity.

Thus some clusters become positive and others negative in order to electrically balance the system.

Figure 17

Here are the main points so far:

Big Bang → waves of energy intersect → tuning → vortex

Basic particles (neutrino, quark, electron) → bonding

Basic structures (proton, neutron) → bonding → atomic nucleus

Atoms

Continuing the above principles, the combined vibration energy emanating from an atomic nucleus would be able to tune with the immediately surrounding lower background energy to form and bond with electrons. So long as this relationship exists, the bonded body of energy (electron+gluon) will be obliged to travel in an orbit around the nucleon's influential field of vibration waves. In other words, as just described, the bonded body (an electron) will experience a **gravitational** force. (Figure 18.)

Electrons, however, are currently explained as being negatively charged and are bound to the positively charged nuclei of atoms by the attraction between opposite electric charges. In a neutral atom the number of electrons is identical to the number of positive charges on the nucleus. At the time of writing I suspected the electric charge of the nucleus may not have been positive but neutral and the electric charge too weak to form a bond with an electron within the outer background lower energy. In addition, I had no direct evidence to indicate the electron was negatively charged.

Nevertheless, both of the above explanations would allow the protons and neutrons surrounded by their attached electrons to remain connected conserving this energy. In this way the atom had, in effect, arranged shared accommodation with its neighbouring electrons. This arrangement was actually necessary within an energy environment subject to ever lowering levels of free high energy. It was in this environment, I suspected, that the first atoms with their cloud of remotely attached electrons were formed (Figure 18).

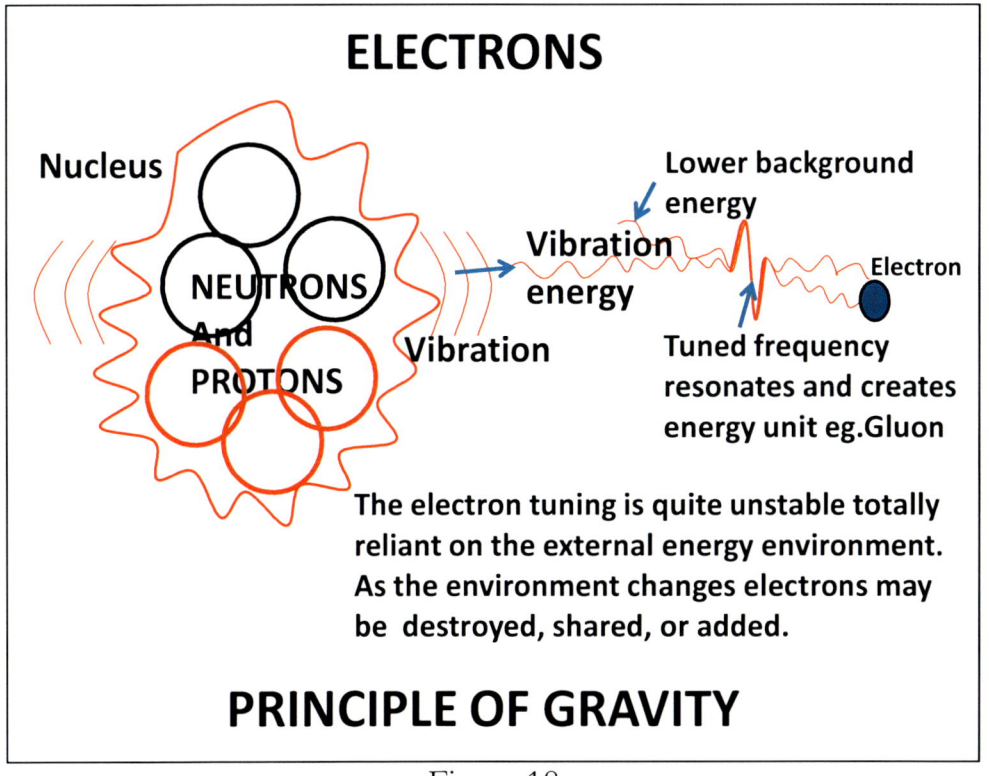

Figure 18

The addition of electrons yielded a host of known atomic varieties, each identifiable and distinguished by a nucleus with a specific number of protons and neutrons together with the number of associated electrons in orbit around the nucleus. However, the surrounding lower energy environment can be constantly changing as atoms compete for the required balance of electrons. Sometimes electrons are shared and sometimes they are lost to other atoms. The continued existence of the electron is very much reliant on the outside background wave energy remaining stable in order for the vibration wave from the nucleus to resonate. Should this change, the bond might be lost, and the electron disappear. This would create an imbalance for the atomic structure until a new electron is secured from elsewhere around the nucleus sphere of influence.

Thus the electromagnetic wave associated with the electron appears to be quite weak and malleable which consequently allows electrons to appear and disappear according to demand. As a result their precise behavior is very unpredictable, a phenomena which enters the realm, and forms the basis of, **Quantum Mechanics**.

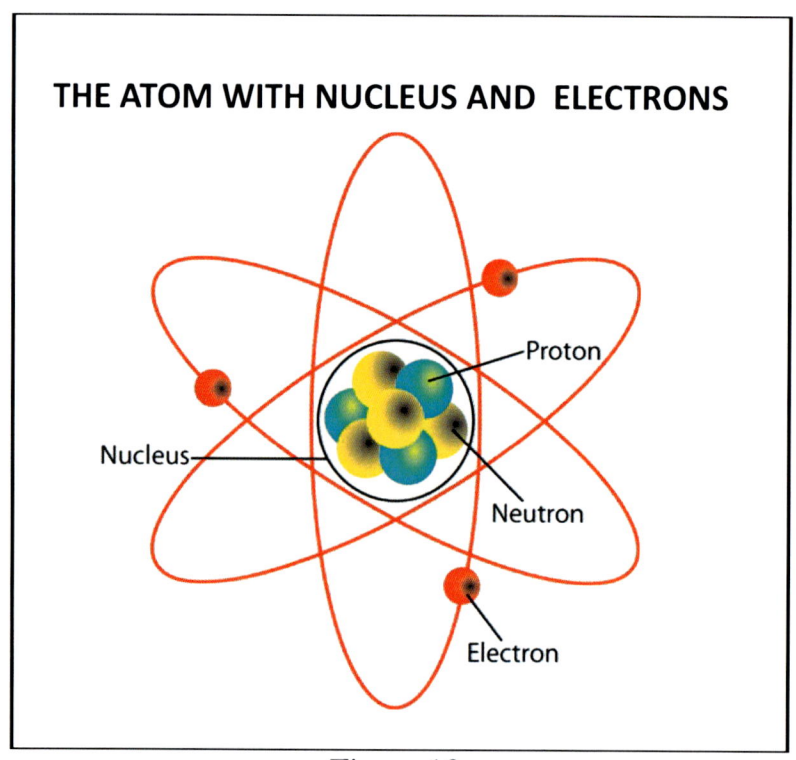

Figure 19

> Basic structures → atomic nucleus (protons, neutrons) → bonding with electrons → complete atom with loosely attached electrons, stored energy of the Big Bang's energy waves

The atom now effectively stores energy. As a consequence of preserving the highest energy within basic particles, the available free energy within our Universe would have lowered, and thus, lower-energy structures with shared particles would now be the favoured structure. Within this new low-energy environment, sharing electrons allowed the building of new energy-saving structures. In this way, and in association with other atoms, they could survive and maintain their original high-energy state. Most importantly, energy would have been continually stored and conserved.

> Energy-saving structures are very important to our existence

The above process of particle construction may well describe the most important factor controlling our existence. Without the 'harmonic resonance' and the consequent bonding mechanisms, together with the high-energy vortex it provides, energy could not be saved and conserved. Otherwise, energy would have continued to travel outwards and dissipate, reducing the Universe to a flash of light. Obviously in such a circumstance, we could not exist.

These early atoms may have been initially small and light, such as hydrogen and helium, and they would have been able to form, and continue to form, so long as there was sufficient high energy in the environment to do so. Once again, following this concept, as the available background energy in the Universe is used and conserved within particles, the remaining amount of available free energy would be lowered.

Molecules and larger structures

Particle construction would consequently adapt and lower-energy constructions such as molecules preferentially generated (Figure 20). Included were large molecular structures such as proteins (e.g. amino acids), carbohydrates, lipids and nucleic acids, all based on complex chains of carbon atoms that would eventually

```
AMINO ACID

      R
      |
H2N — C — C — OH
      |   ||
      H   O
```

lead to the development of life.

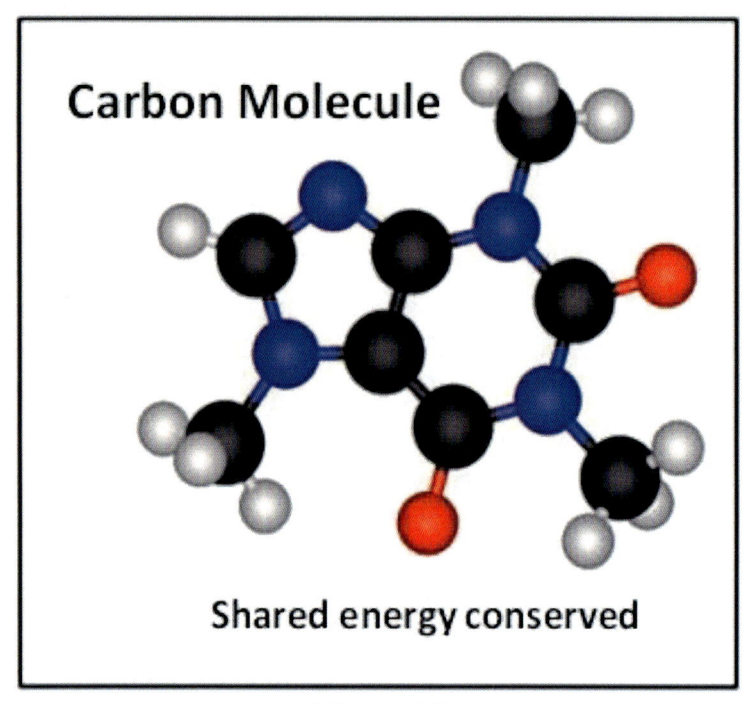

Figure 20

Gravity

As the atoms and molecules go on to build larger and more complex structures with a consequent increase in 'mass'. The Earth was now able to increase its field of vibration and wave influence. This created an ever increasing gravitational force that could tune with ourselves and all other objects and draw them into towards the centre of the Earth. We feel this as weight. This prevents us floating off into space and keeps everything safely on the ground. It thus becomes possible to see how this gravitational force of vibration waves would continue to apply, and that the larger planetary bodies with their dense mass, would also be able to exert a similar gravitational force on the adjacent planets and moons, and why the planets orbit the sun. Given sufficient distance, however, the effect of the vibration waves decrease which we will experience as weightlessness in outer space.

(NB. The Bonding and Gravity mechanisms described above are based on my own personal understanding of these forces. They correspond more closely with Newton's laws of gravity than those proposed by Einstein).

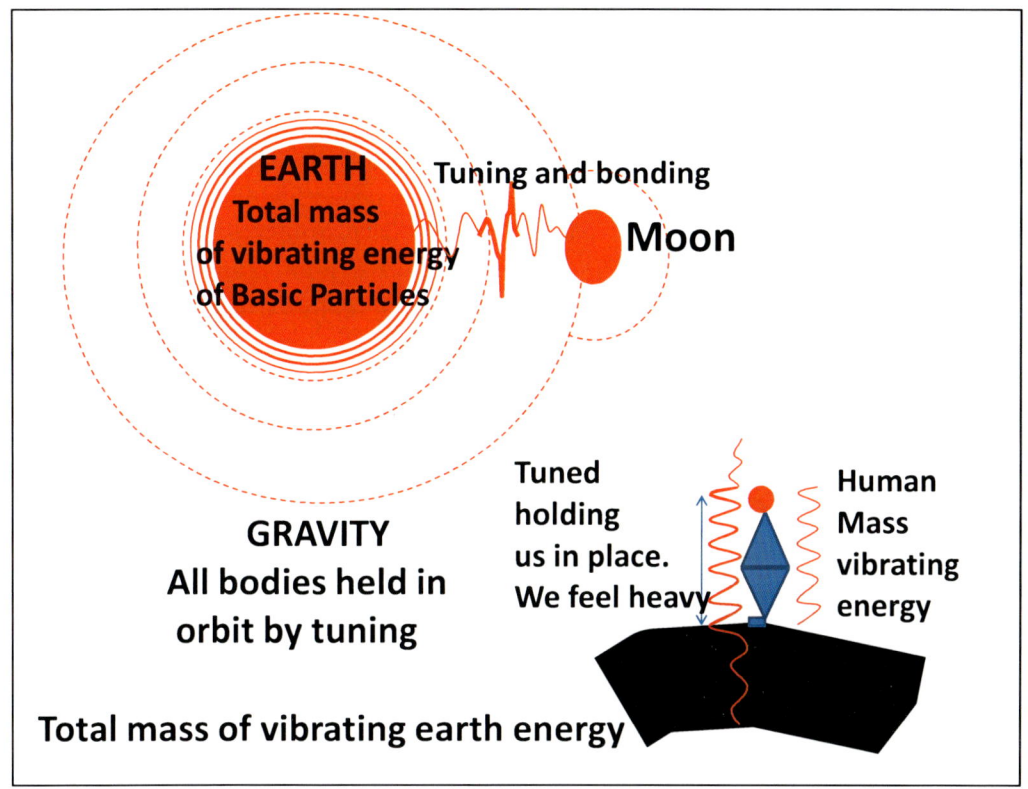

Figure 21

Selfish Universe

The process of construction seems always brutal and mechanical. The nucleus took the electrons as they were needed and when a suitable opportunity arose. It was done, it seems 'selfishly', without regard for the effects on other particles. It didn't care if there was one less magnesium atom in the Universe or whether there was one more atom of copper. It took no note of other atoms and their requirements. It was only content with its own needs; to balance and satisfy the forces. Metaphorically, this could be considered selfish. So why was the need so strong to balance the energy within these structures? I was fascinated by these thoughts, so of course I continued exploring.

Conservation of energy

First, it appears that each atomic, chemical and organic bond locked energy into their structure. In this way it would conserve energy. As discussed, if all these bonds were to be released and returned to the first moments after the Big Bang, Newton's laws of thermodynamics suggest the energy would have dissipated to the lowest state of energy, a process we refer to as 'entropy'. As a consequence, the Universe, with its galaxies and planets, would be reduced, as stated previously, to a flash of light. Fortunately, this had been avoided by the natural properties and behaviour of energy in motion described earlier in this section. These properties initiated and allowed nuclear structures to develop and so conserve energy.

It was important, therefore, to sustain these nuclear structures and to repair any possible imbalances. This maintenance process appeared to be initiated as follows: once a structure was developed, an imbalance would automatically trigger a 'vacancy', which could then be satisfied by any available and suitable unit of energy to restore the balance. It was the same as the need within the organic world to feed. Devouring and destroying other organisms is selfish but necessary to balance our own particular chemical combinations. This vacancy appeared, therefore, to set in motion the need to balance and, at the same time, the need to survive in both inorganic and organic substances. It was the driver of selfishness.

As a consequence energy was constantly being stored within atomic, molecular and organic structures. In fact, the Universe appeared to be obsessed with the conservation of energy, and as a result, and fortunately for us and the Universe, entropy (the dissipation of energy) is delayed. However, what advantage was being offered, other than delaying the inevitable entropy? Will entropy prevail? Or won't it?

I suspected the answer may lie within relationships with adjacent parallel universes. Perhaps our Universe might exist in a relationship with other adjacent and parallel universes in the same way that atoms co-exist side-by-side with other atoms. For example, imagine that an atom represents a single universe. This hypothetical universe would manage its energy in the same way as our Universe, just as an atom maintains internal integrity by close management of its internal energy resources. However, an atom also requires, from time to time, to borrow or share electrons with other adjacent atoms in order to balance and maintain stability. At a higher order, couldn't this have been the situation with our own Universe? Perhaps stellar explosions, black hole development, anti-matter formation within our Universe might create energy imbalances and facilitate required energy exchanges between adjacent universe systems.

Within our Universe, there appeared to be three quite distinct energy levels associated with nuclear construction, which I informally refer to as Templates (Figure 22):

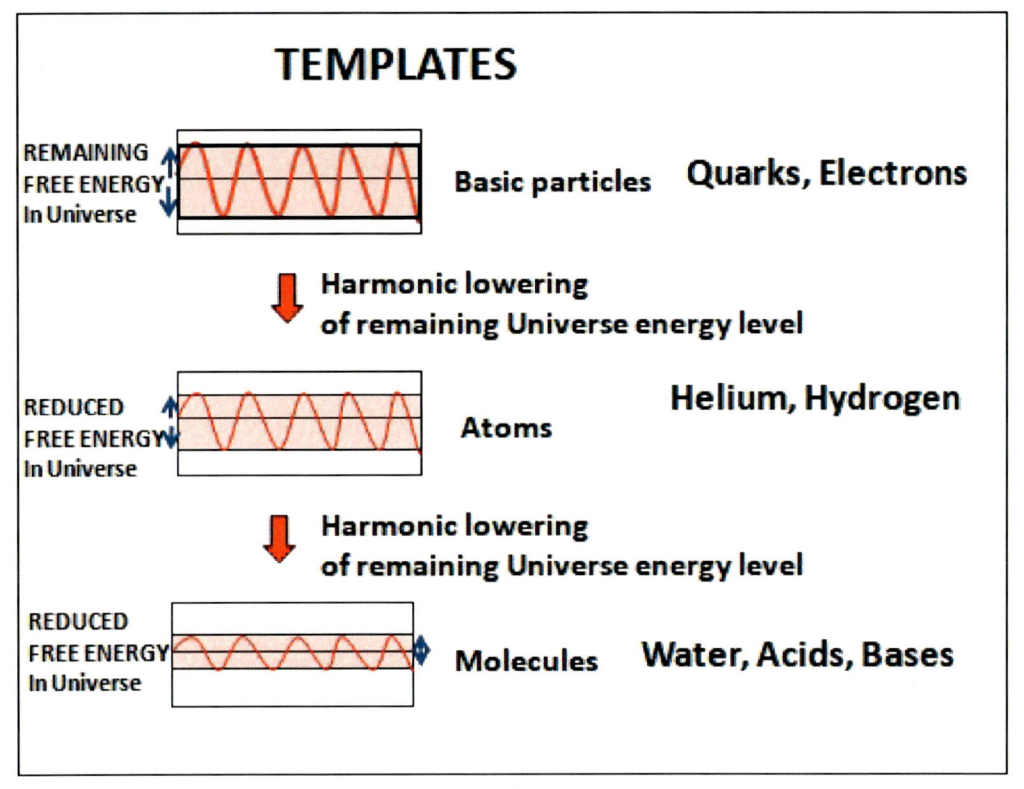

Figure 22: How the Universe conserves energy with various structures.

Template 1   Highest level: quarks, neutrinos, electrons.

Template 2   Mid-level: protons, neutrons, shared electrons and atom formation.

Template 3   Lower level: molecular construction,

An additional high energy template could also be considered, represented by Dark Energy. As the Big Bang was initiated, its entire content of energy was able to resonate, both positive 'in phase' and neutral 'out of phase' energy. I believe the former positive 'in phase' maxima may have had detectable polarity and momentum which became clear in the early particles such as the quarks (Figure 23).

The latter 'out of phase' energy would have no detectable momentum or polarity since its electromagnetic energy had been neutralised and would remain as potential energy in relatively motionless, inactive, amorphous clouds. I refer to these clouds as **dark energy**. In the absence of polarity the clouds would be free to float around the galaxies, virtually undetectable without any interaction with positive 'in phase' matter (see figure 23).

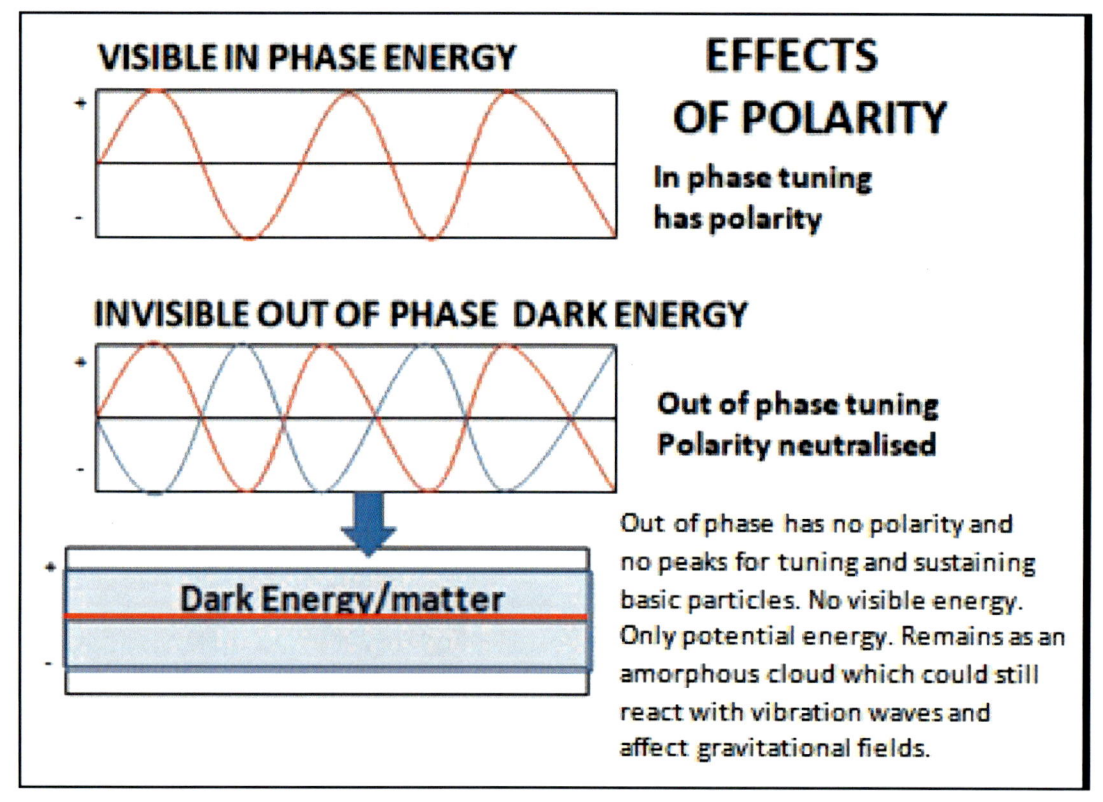

Figure 23

Multiple universes and the Universal Force
The above Templates imply a predictable evolution of energy management within our Universe and thus would develop in a predictable manner. As a consequence, this could be true for adjacent universes. It follows that for any universe to exist, it almost demands the presence of adjacent parallel universes to share and properly manage its own energy resources. At the same time, if this is true, sharing energy with adjacent universes would slow the process of dissipation and entropy.

Similarly, if the above is true, then it would also imply consequences for Newton's laws of thermodynamics. Within our own Universe, particles were simply responding to the most fundamental *force* of the Universe (and probably all universes) described in Newton's first two laws of thermodynamics. Such a *Universal Force* supposedly ensured that the bank balance of energy within the Universe was maintained. Simply stated, the first law requires that the Universe was a contained system with a fixed amount of energy and in which this energy could neither be added to nor destroyed. The second law suggests that such contained systems in isolation spontaneously tend toward greater disorganisation, that complex higher-energy forms would degrade and divide into lower-energy forms that were simpler, a process known as 'entropy'. However, as described above, imbalances occur at atomic levels and could also occur at a cosmic level in association with, for example, stellar explosions. On such occasions, the Universe might develop a slight surplus or deficit of free energy. This notion appeared to contradict Newton's 'fixed amount of energy in the bank account'. It would thus have to share or selfishly take energy from adjacent universes – an intriguing thought.

I also dared to think of an origin for our Universe. Where did it come from and why? One possible explanation could have employed the same mechanisms that created the basic particles. I imagined that outside the present Universe, we are surrounded by a vast, endless churning ocean of energy waves, constantly oscillating and which could occasionally intersect and tune to form a giant Standing Wave, a process identical to the Standing Wave that created the quark and neutrino. This unit which had increased momentum would separate and spiral into a vortex with immense energy to create its own self-contained, possibly rotating, universe. Suddenly, I now realised that the formation of our Universe may not have been accompanied by a 'Big Bang'. Effectively the Universe would be now floating 'quietly' within this vast ocean of energy.

The above process could go on to create other Standing Waves and more universes all similarly floating freely within this ocean. Extrapolating this model further, perhaps the energy vibration caused by the vortex would allow tuning with adjacent universes, (as with quarks) and cause each universe to bond with those adjacent. Thus I could imagine they might even cluster to form what would be an analogue to a gigantic nucleus. My imagination was now running riot with further extensions of this evolution, but I stopped for fear of ridicule. These were just speculative thoughts. However, these ideas did present support for the notion that we are not the only Universe. Here was a mechanism to explain this was likely.

Notice how I employed and emphasised the term 'selfish' and 'sharing' with regard to non-organic, lifeless particles. I am sure a few of the readers will take exception to this use of descriptive terminology normally reserved for human activity. How could we say inorganic particles have human-like qualities? Well, in fact, I believed **metaphorically** they did because they are the same particles that make up our body, and as just explained, they are the same particles that are directly involved in causing us, as humans, to behave selfishly. Simply viewed, the mechanics of human emotion and the driving force of all human activity, is created from the requirement of our particular atomic and molecular composition to maintain and satisfy its balance of gravitational and electrical forces. We will do all we 'selfishly' can to ensure this happens. It is my opinion that this is why we exist. This thirst for particles to maintain a chemical balance and harmony, together with the natural *force* to sustain the equilibrium between mass and energy, led to the same selfish *force* that is inherited and operates in humans. There is no physical difference between what happens within the *Universal Force* at the basic atomic level and the *force* for contentment within the human body. This is the *force* we all feel within us – our inner spiritual drive. So I hope the reader will forgive my use of such 'human' terminology again to describe apparently inanimate chemical processes.

Having established in my mind a possible origin of selfishness, I turned my attention from the microscopic to the larger, macroscopic scale of our planet and the origin of life.

7

THE DEVELOPMENT OF LIFE

Prior to this time, the surface of our newly formed planet would have been barren, formed of volcanic rock together with an atmosphere rich in ammonia and sulphur. Water was only just beginning to condense on to the Earth's surface provided by the massive invasion of meteorites at this early time. Only at this stage would the rivers begin to flow and create lakes and seas, provided by the supply of water from the ice and rock of the meteorites and comets.

(NB. The evolution of our particular solar system at this particular time is believed to have allowed more meteorite impacts during these early stages of planet development.)

With this final ingredient water, new types of molecules arose that eventually resembled those for life. Life would make the first attempts to form in this sort of environment. However, at this early stage, the process might have only been random, vaguely steered by the need of chemically imbalanced molecules to be balanced by others. Certain elements would be selected and combine that could eventually proceed towards organic life. So, as always, I asked which elements were selected and why.

It was well documented that the Earth's crust was made mostly of oxygen, silicon, aluminium, sodium, calcium, iron, magnesium and potassium. Living tissues, however, were made predominantly of hydrogen, oxygen, carbon and nitrogen, with the rest of the elements adding up to less than 1 percent of the total. It was noticeable, therefore, that the complexities of life did not evolve out of the most common elements but instead out of a select few. It would fall to these weakly charged and loosely bonded atoms of carbon, hydrogen, nitrogen and the limited supply of oxygen to provide the useful source material necessary to build the complex and flexible molecules for life. But the molecules they initially formed would almost certainly have been simple structures, and this was not life.

It is one thing to say these elements went on to build living organisms but quite another to actually take these elements into a laboratory and do it. Science, at this time, was littered with attempts by scientists and the authors of science fiction to create life from these apparently inanimate chemicals. Life isn't that simple. But then life wasn't built in a day, as it was by the fictional Frankenstein. It would need time to cook a little.

I would wander around the university complex, trying to visualise just how all these random molecular structures could arrive in the right place at the right time. There seemed to be a lot of fortuitous events required at this stage for this to happen.

In my mind, I had images of hot geysers along the edges of the seas which would bubble and explode like a giant cauldron cooking up this mysterious chemical experiment; an alchemy of alchemies. Could these cauldrons have provided the energy and allowed the available elements to combine and form the multitude of different and varied molecular structures required?

One point to be borne in mind, I realised, was that the physical composition of water offers an ideal medium to bring the vital ingredients together. The tetrahedrons that H_2O forms are actually spacious for the hydrogen and oxygen atoms to position themselves within the ionic forces. There was enough room within the central part of these particular pyramidal structures to accommodate other elements, such as carbon, nitrogen and others, without chemically bonding. In other words, they could have easily absorbed elements and then given them up if warmed or mixed with other more interactive solutions. For example, the process of dissolving aspirin in water or mixing the coloured elemental substances we used to paint our watercolour pictures. The water absorbed the substances, yet they remained chemically distinct. The water was still H_2O water; it did not alter its chemical structure. This 'solubility' was a property of water most of us were familiar with and took for granted. However, in the early stages of this alchemy, it was an important property, for it allowed a variety of rarer, as well as common, elements to be captured and brought together.

In addition, it could also have been the case that the newly arrived clay minerals washed in from the recently formed rivers provided a tool to shape and steer the otherwise random construction process. It had been suggested that the weak ionic electrical forces inherent in the platy and layered nature of the clay internal molecular structures may have influenced the alignment of the weaker carbon molecules. This way, the electrical forces consequently operating on these platy surfaces could have provided a sort of template for the design of repeatable organic molecular structures and possibly shaped long strands of nucleotides. It would then have been a small step to develop a simple single-strand chromosome.

The present-day RNA was a key molecule at this early stage that was able to form a single-strand chromosome and store genetic information as well as to catalyse chemical reactions. This, together with the fluids being confined within the tiny pore spaces of the newly deposited silt and mudstones, may have provided an ideal environment to begin the chemical evolutionary process of organic life-like molecules. Furthermore, deep-sea settings were relatively undisturbed and could have received additional energy in the form of heat from geothermal fumaroles and chemicals such as energy-rich iron and hydrogen sulphides.

But what sort of chemicals could freely form within these newly forming volcanic and deep-sea environments? And would these be useful to kick start the process of life?

Clearly carbon molecules would be essential ingredients to any 'start-up' process. It was an element that had many attractive properties for such a purpose. Carbon was capable of reacting with 'electronegative' elements like oxygen, nitrogen, phosphorous, sulphur and chlorine as well as the 'electropositive' element hydrogen. Carbon was also capable of forming single, double and triple bonds with other carbon atoms. These could form a relatively strong and durable chain, with ring and branched networks. These could have a variety of chemical properties. It seemed likely, therefore, that the most stable organic-like structures generated in these varying conditions would have been various types of carbon-bonded molecules. From these simple varieties of carbon molecules, amino acids, an essential ingredient of proteins, a basic building block for life, could have evolved. Without these amino acids, life couldn't begin.

These were the early organic molecules in the making but, there were still difficulties to overcome. It seemed likely the molecular process was more or less random, only able to sustain basic, simple molecules, and most of these may have been varieties of acids. Any attempts at building other types of life-sustaining organic molecules would probably have been hampered by variations in the composition and temperature of the water, thus altering and perhaps destroying the newly bonded structures. Such cycles of building and destruction may have existed for millions of years within the early primordial seas. In addition, the so-called primordial soup may have actually been more comparable to consommé than the rich broth we think of today. In such an environment, the weak concentration of any candidate life-sustaining molecules may have been too rare and isolated to meet up with other suitable candidate molecules. Even those fluids trapped within sediment pores may not have been that rich in essential ingredients. As a consequence, one could imagine that chemical evolution towards life may have been rather slow at this stage, that is, until by relative chance a particular combination of molecules and atoms, referred to as RNA and particularly DNA (distinguished by the added oxygen in RNA), arranged themselves in a chain in such a way that other molecules and atoms could be added alongside each other to build an identical copy of this same structure. Employing the single nucleotide strands of RNA, a chromosome structure could be evolved. It wasn't until the arrival of this new type of chemical template in the form of RNA that life as we know it could begin. From here, it appeared, evolved all life.

I remember in one of my early biology lectures I was shocked to hear that RNA-DNA form the basis for all life forms. There appears to be no other structure we can call life. (I was also shocked, during a biology practical, to see one of the biology students collapse at the side of me, when her dissected beautiful white rabbit came alive and was trying to pull away from the pins that held it in place. I also remember the smell of formalin, the specimen preservative, which seemed to linger for hours after each practical and on into lunch. Hmm.)

Returning to the earliest life forms, I understood that viruses were based on single-strand RNA nucleotides made up of a five-carbon ribose sugar, a phosphate molecule and one of four nitrogenous bases which could include adenine, guanine, cytosine or uracil (see Figure 24a). This chemical association could have formed one of the first organic life forms, possibly before bacteria or eukaryotes. Being the only form of life, a parasitic virus could feed off other virus structures and use their constituents to reproduce, together with nutrients absorbed from within the primordial sea. Note immediately the 'selfish' behaviour that seemed inherent in this process. However, the unsavoury selfish nature of the parasitic virus I could not dismiss; it would have been a valuable survival mechanism which would have enabled a prolific expansion and growth of organic life.

(Post-1995, since the writing of this original manuscript, several publications have confirmed the likelihood of such possibilities. They are summarised in the book by Richard Egel et al. (2006) and which include articles by Martin and Koonin et al. (2006) and Forterre and Prangishvili (2006).)

The RNA virus, however, had only the single self-replicating chromosome. If there were individuals with errors, the errors were copied. Mutation was exponential. DNA was a double-stranded chromosome which was able to ignore a damaged gene by reproducing the correct version during reproduction. Mutation was slower, but it was still, with its inherent, parasitic nature, a very efficient self-replicating molecule and was still essentially a virus. I could now envisage the living organic world was born.

DNA would have been more stable and thus became more and more essential to the continuation of life. Literature indicated the constituent building blocks of DNA (see Figures 24b and 24c) consisted of phosphates, sugars and nitrogen bases held in pairs: the now famous adenine–thymine (AT) and guanine–cytosine (GC) pairs. **DNA** was a very large molecule of deoxyribonucleic acid, a double helix made up of two separate strands of DNA, represented by phosphoric acid and pentose sugars(=deoxyribose), twisted around each other (S). The double stranded structure was stabilised by its attached nitrogen bases which pointed inwards and could form hydrogen bonds between the coiling DNA strands carrying the genetic code (see diagrams, Figure 24c). This way, they could build to form a twisted rope ladder with solid rungs. In figure 24b and 24c the DNA is not twisted. These long and often multiple strands represent **nucleotides**. Within these nucleotide strands are particular areas suspected as initiating molecular construction and thus become known as gene-associated regions and thus referred to as **genes**. These genes make up different DNA sequences called **genotypes**. Together with their attached bases, they can extend to extreme lengths to form **chromosomes**. The DNA in one chromosome could actually comprise hundreds of thousands of nucleotides and bases. The genes within represent the cell's nuclear **genome** and act as the control centre of the cell. The current model for DNA suggests it is able to construct these bonds in any order or sequence, thus placing no particular restriction on the sequence in which the base pairs follow each other. This means in practice a DNA molecule can be any size and combination of adenine–thymine and guanine–cytosine bonds.

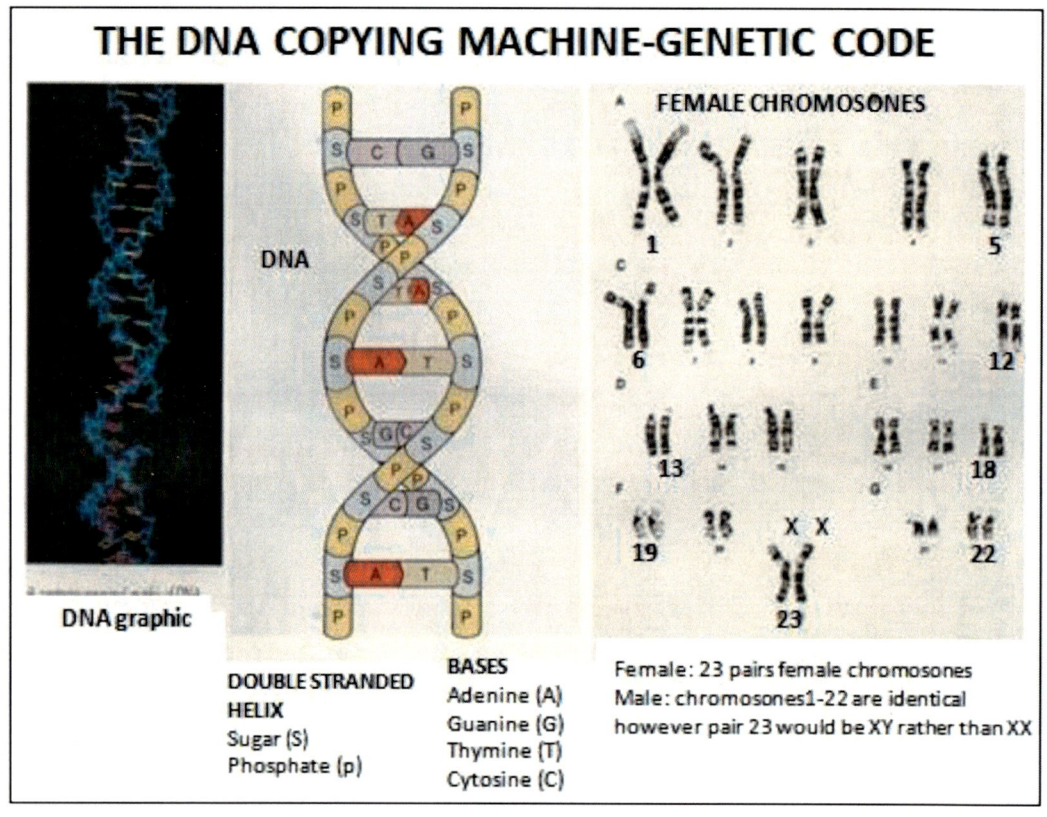

Figure 24a

This clever association of sugars, phosphate and nitrogen bases together with the inherited parasitic nature, referred to as DNA, provided a timeless and perfect replicating device which could enable all organic molecular structures to be copied and reproduced (Figure 24b).

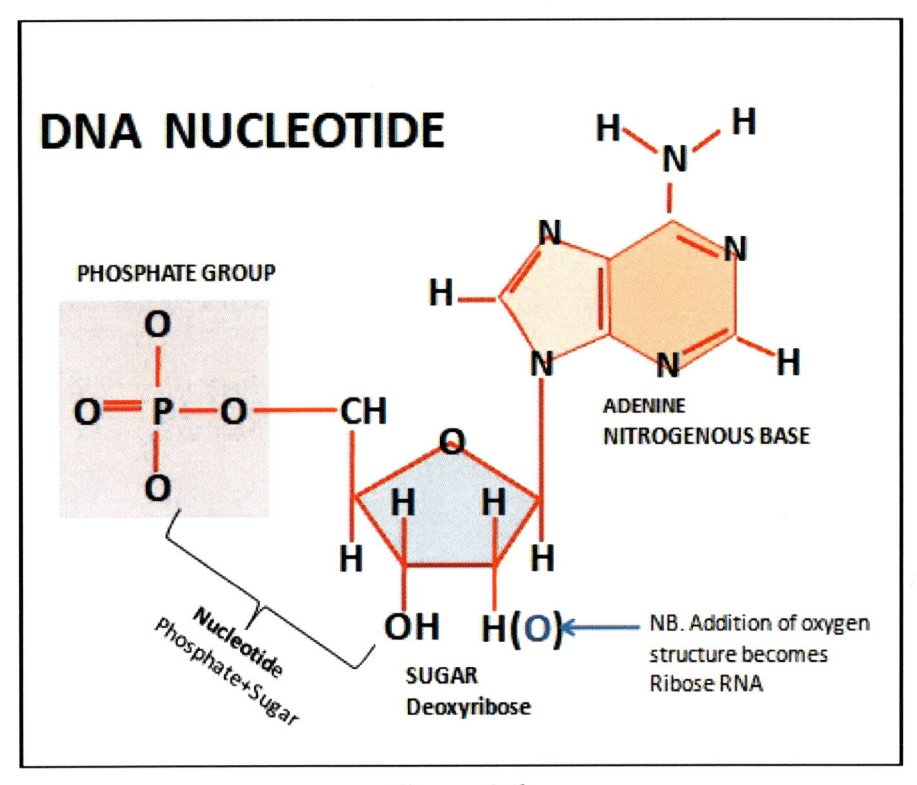

Figure 24b

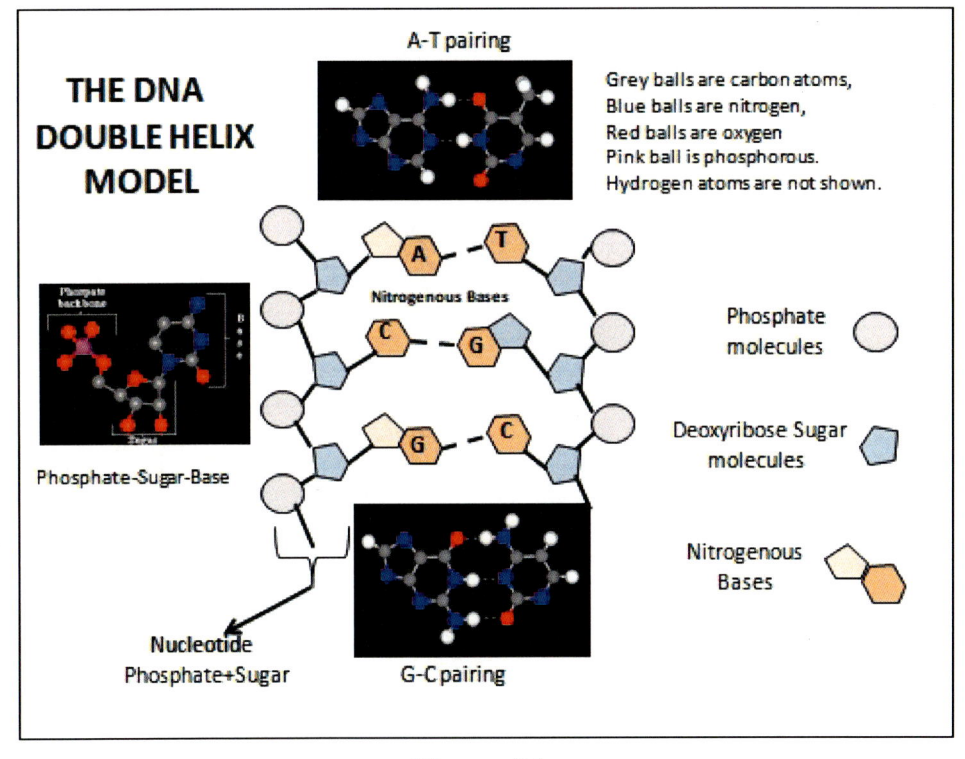

Figure 24c

This particular combination and arrangement of the minute variations could be saved as a code and incorporated, as a genetic code, thus providing a mechanism to accelerate the reproduction of successful forms able to survive. It was a development that enabled organic evolution to progress more rapidly than ever before and thus could extend the construction cycle much further than before.

It was thus vital that the replicating molecule DNA, and their genetic code, survived and continued. Over time, these units became more organised and more complex, eventually able to synthesise membranes for their cell walls. The consequent cell system would enable the replicating device to survive. The genes within represented the cell's nuclear genome and acted as the control centre of the cell (Figure 25).

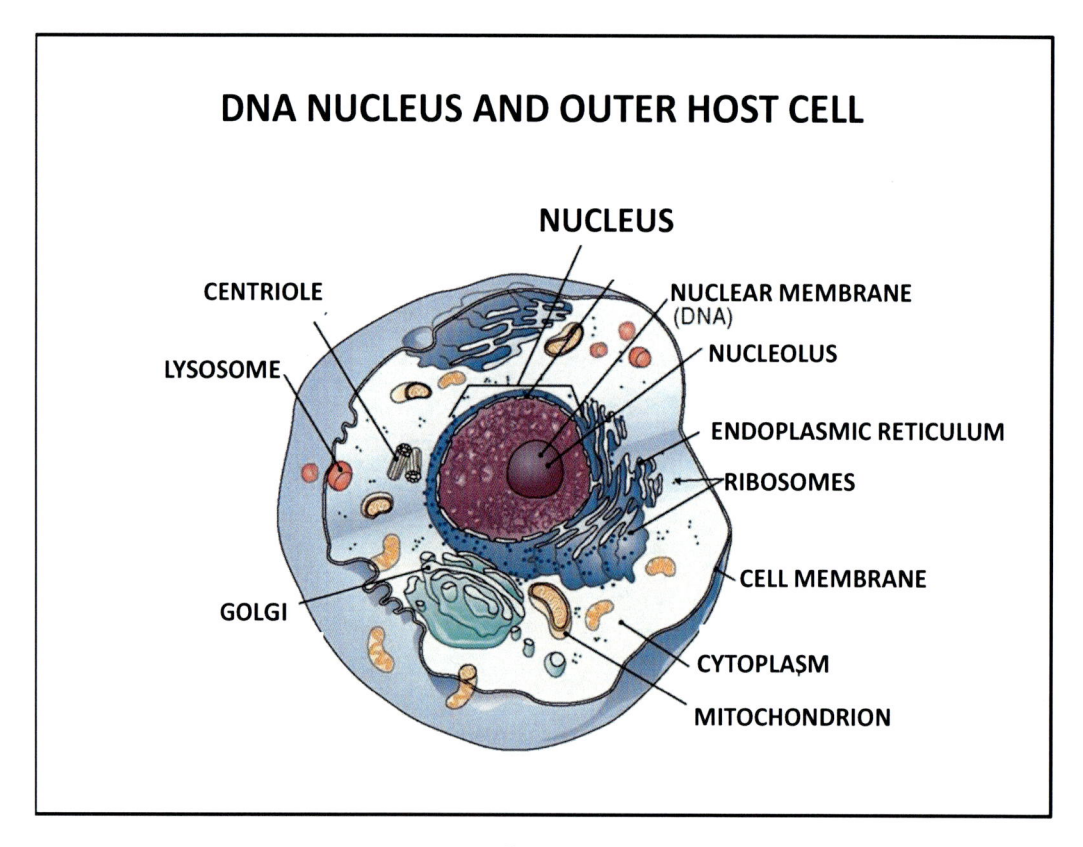

Figure 25

This information made me realise that with DNA at their centre, this self-perpetuating system allowed an almost limitless growth of these new molecules. This living system, that is, the DNA code with the surrounding cell, could thus provide itself with an ideal vehicle to be protected and survive. The security of DNA was more or less assured. Except, however, its survival now depended on the survival of the outer cell and that the survival of the outer cell was now also paramount.

Unfortunately, the individual cells would also eventually destruct because of the long-term impact of polluting chemicals and errors in molecular replication, damaging the component constituents of the cell. In essence, the protective cellular vehicle grew old and died. To avoid these long-term problems and the likely extermination it could bring, DNA, and its inherent code, allowed the whole virus system to divide and be replicated at its optimum stage of growth, that is, its maturity. These replicas contained the code and now represented the new vehicles to be nurtured and cared for, as they carried forward, blindly and selfishly with the ever-thirsty construction cycle. The whole nature of the virus we know today, such as the flu virus, appeared 'selfish', with their hard-driven desire to replicate to the cost of our health. However, without this selfish desire, immediate extinction of DNA would have been almost certain.

Armed with this innate ability to reproduce, it seemed likely, even at this very early stage of development, that the inherent code (the genetic code) within this virus-like DNA molecule, may have had more or less full control of the 'host' cellular contents. We know from the present activities of DNA that it signals the construction of various types of proteins for hormones and other molecular activity within the cell.

I thus believed that with cellular advancement and the increasing complexity of the DNA within the nucleus, the detailed code was probably able to communicate and so steer the activity of the 'host outer cellular material' by responding to electro-chemical information about its surrounding conditions and triggering an appropriate response, not only within the short range of its own cell but also in longer-range adjacent cells (Figure 26). This direct-response mechanism from any one individual cell to another was probably limited. However, I surmised the collective effect of the many thousands of slightly different cellular DNA responses may have triggered the required stimulus that would ultimately lead to the direct steering and control of the host organism's cellular activities. Hence, the genetic code of DNA, protected within the inner nucleus of the cell, may thus have a direct influence upon the activities of their host outer cells. Consequently, every moment of the individual life form's existence could be controlled by the DNA within the nucleus and focused towards its primary and solitary purpose, that is, the survival of DNA 'itself' and its inherent genetic code.

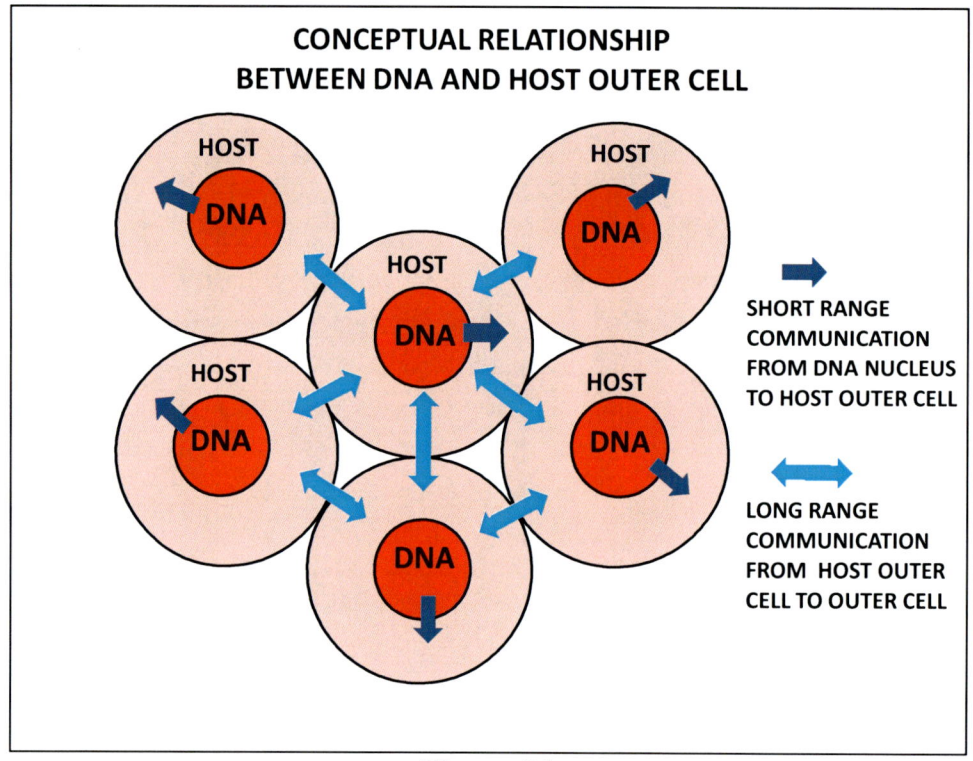

Figure 26

As discussed earlier, another curious but important process was happening here besides the origin of life. To sustain these new organic structures within the laws of thermodynamics, the structures would be subject to the process of entropy. It would result in the eventual breakdown into units with lower levels of energy, conforming to the gradual dissipation of energy consequent in all other natural processes. The almost magical appearance of DNA had changed all this. Its eventual development of the cell and its specialised organelles enabled energy to be absorbed even from the sun's ultraviolet rays. In photosynthesis, plants used the energy from light to convert carbon dioxide and water into organic materials, which are the building blocks of living organisms. This way, the cell, instead of losing energy, could gain energy and thus modify and delay the effects of entropy.

The separate emergence of the organic molecule mitochondrion and its ultimate combination with the cell provided additional energy and allowed the simple cell to quickly diversify into those that used mitochondria and chloroplasts to gain additional energy directly from the sun (prokaryotes) and those that employed mitochondria alone to provide energy (eukaryotes). The chloroplast limited their cells to the plant kingdom. They went on to develop phytoplankton, seaweeds, liverworts, ferns, trees and flowering plants. The mitochondria also allowed energy to be absorbed by ingesting organic material from the chloroplast forms and breaking this down to release the energy. The eukaryotes thus went on to eventually develop the animal kingdom. Ultimately the animal kingdom relied on the prokaryotes for food. For example, herbivores eat vegetation, and carnivores eat herbivores.

Life thus evolved stage by stage, each organism selfishly competing with its neighbours for survival and a chance to reproduce within an environment of limited resources. Those who were suited best to the local environment would most likely survive. Those that were not would perish. Any slight changes in the shape or form of the organism that subsequently proved advantageous allowed that organism a greater chance in the competition for survival. This competition had led the most basic single cells to combine and form multicellular forms, to develop into fish, amphibians, reptiles, mammals and eventually man. In our case, the development of the brain and intellect had given us the ultimate survival advantage.

The complex forms this mechanism has managed to evolve so far are summarised and illustrated in Figure 27.

All these life forms had successfully passed on the genetic code and therefore allowed life to continue. It seemed to me, as such, these life forms merely provided a host, a temporary home and safe haven for the genetic code. They, including all of us, were merely complex vehicles, a host, suitably equipped with inbuilt safety and security features, allowing the continuous replication of these very early and primeval DNA molecules: the molecules which carried the genetic code.

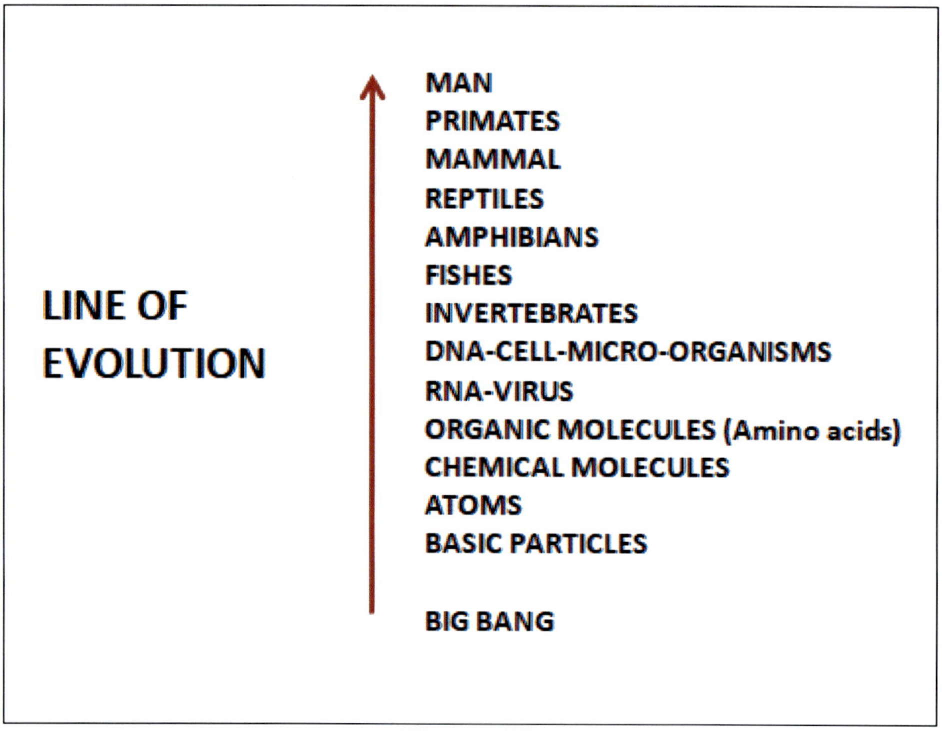

```
                    ↑  MAN
                       PRIMATES
                       MAMMAL
                       REPTILES
                       AMPHIBIANS
                       FISHES
  LINE OF              INVERTEBRATES
                       DNA-CELL-MICRO-ORGANISMS
  EVOLUTION            RNA-VIRUS
                       ORGANIC MOLECULES (Amino acids)
                       CHEMICAL MOLECULES
                       ATOMS
                       BASIC PARTICLES

                       BIG BANG
```

Figure 27

So here I had appreciated yet one more facet of this selfishness. It was not only directed towards our own survival but more importantly towards the nurture and survival of our children, the carriers of future DNA. It was imperative for the survival of the genetic code that it is passed on into new, younger vehicles. I now appreciated that the previous cycle of molecular construction and destruction had now been broken. With the help of new energy from the sun via the chloroplast, and the mitochondria, construction could continue infinitely. It could survive to build even more complex and sophisticated structures, its only limitation being the requirement to pass on DNA. This additional energy from the sun ultimately ensured not only the survival of the genetic code but also organic life, which in turn delayed the destructive process of entropy and allowed more energy to be generated and conserved in our Universe. Failure to reproduce and pass on the code would rapidly lead to the collapse of the organic system and a return to the simple carbon molecular non-life systems prior to the arrival of DNA. Life, as we know it, would have disappeared and our planet would be returned to a barren dusty surface. Security of DNA and its continuation into the future was paramount. This is why I believed that everything we do is selfish and directed towards our survival.

Even our most brave and charitable acts appear guilty of being selfish (as well as uncharitable acts). It's hard to believe that in its own way an uncharitable act is a more honest statement of intention than the deviously disguised charity. The worst is to realise that when we smile, our DNA is in actual fact attempting to pacify our fellow human beings to secure our own position. This is the *Life Force*, driven by the *Universal Force,* at its simplest – selfish and brutal, a harsh reality to digest.

This is why (referring back to our original story) I suspected the heroic acts of the mother were purely selfish deeds driven by the instinctive requirements of DNA. The mother, by attempting to save the child, was only selfishly trying to protect the 'future' of her own genetic code at any cost. Her own aging DNA-copying machine could be discarded in such times of crisis in preference for the survival of her child, the new and younger vehicle. (Please note that I employ the word 'selfish' to illustrate the 'vacancy' process described earlier.. It is not intended as a moral judgement).

8

THE GREY MATTER

Selfishness and survival
The survival of the DNA genetic code and life
The tripartite system controls and ensures our survival

Now despite all I had learned concerning the relationship between DNA and selfishness, this understanding still had not given me a clear explanation of what controlled happiness and what caused happiness to be so elusive. My earlier philosophising told me that provided I behaved within the moral boundaries of my immediate environment, I could expect to be content, and that if I strayed outside these boundaries, I could expect to meet discomfort. The obvious relationship between DNA, selfishness and survival, the drive to pass on the code, I had established. Our selfish behaviour can be seen as an important parameter in all life's activities and as such must play their part in our emotional condition. That our happiness was in some way linked to this lay tantalisingly before me, but the precise nature of this link was not that obvious. I had now researched the origins of the Earth and life to find some of the basic physics and biochemistry that may underlie the nature of our behaviour. This all yielded clues. Yet there was clearly something else.

So many features of this condition known as 'happiness' remained unexplained. For instance, when I had achieved a happy state of mind, why couldn't I keep it that way? If I was on holiday, for example, in my favourite place of relaxation, why was it I could still feel grumpy one day and happy another? It didn't tell me why, after receiving a lot of money, I might feel unhappy a few hours later. In addition 'contentment' seemed to be an experience that was neither very happy nor sad. It was a pleasant, almost neutral state of mind in which we, perhaps, spend most of our time. All of this needed explanation.

Other areas of pleasurable experience also puzzled me. These were more abstract and vague. For example, it didn't tell me why listening to a particular piece of music could make me feel so happy. I was particularly intrigued by this last question since at this time I spent quite a lot of my time experimenting with different themes and tunes on the piano. Each of the halls in the college had a piano. I would always steal as much time as possible to play. I was not a gifted piano player, no such luck, and everything I played was by 'ear'. It was a limited style, but for whatever reason, I needed to play. To discover a new chord sequence, a new syncopation, was thrilling. Nearly all the music I played was original but only in the sense that I didn't know how to play other people's tunes and I was too impatient to learn. So each time I played depended very much on how I felt that day. It would be a voyage of discovery, feeling for new or interesting sounds and themes whilst holding to established safe and harmonious areas. I didn't care if I was bad or good; I needed to play like I needed food. It was just great therapy, or at least it appeared to me that way. I could weave day-to-day emotions into a tapestry of sound, almost as if entering thoughts into a diary. I could be happy or sad. It could move me to tears – tears of joy or tears of pain. But I had no clear idea of why or how. This medium didn't appear to have any obvious biological function. Even more intriguing is that almost no other creature appeared to employ sound in this manner. Yet this abstract area of 'music', with no apparent and obvious biological function, was intimately involved in the way I felt.

And what about all the other abstract areas of activity such as painting, stage performances or art? All these had the same non-biological status. Obviously the controls on our emotional condition were many and complex, and many fundamental questions remained unanswered before I could begin to understand my principal enquiry – the controls of happiness and contentment.

This wasn't the sort of progress I wanted. The problem was where to search next. At this stage, I decided to turn my attention to more fully understanding the brain, the organ that has provided human beings with their ultimate survival advantage. Without some proper understanding of how this complex structure functioned, I really couldn't proceed. This, however, was a considerable challenge. I knew the basics from my courses in biology at university. Additional literature that was comprehensible seemed hard to find in the 1960s and the early 1970s. To start, I would have to settle for the basic textbooks.

The first thing I learned was that there were two basic parts to the brain: the older reptilian brain, incorporated and surrounded by the limbic system, and the more recent cerebral cortex, which forms an outer layer over the old reptilian brain as shown in Figure 28.

COMPONENTS OF LIMBIC SYSTEM AND THE OLD REPTILIAN BRAIN

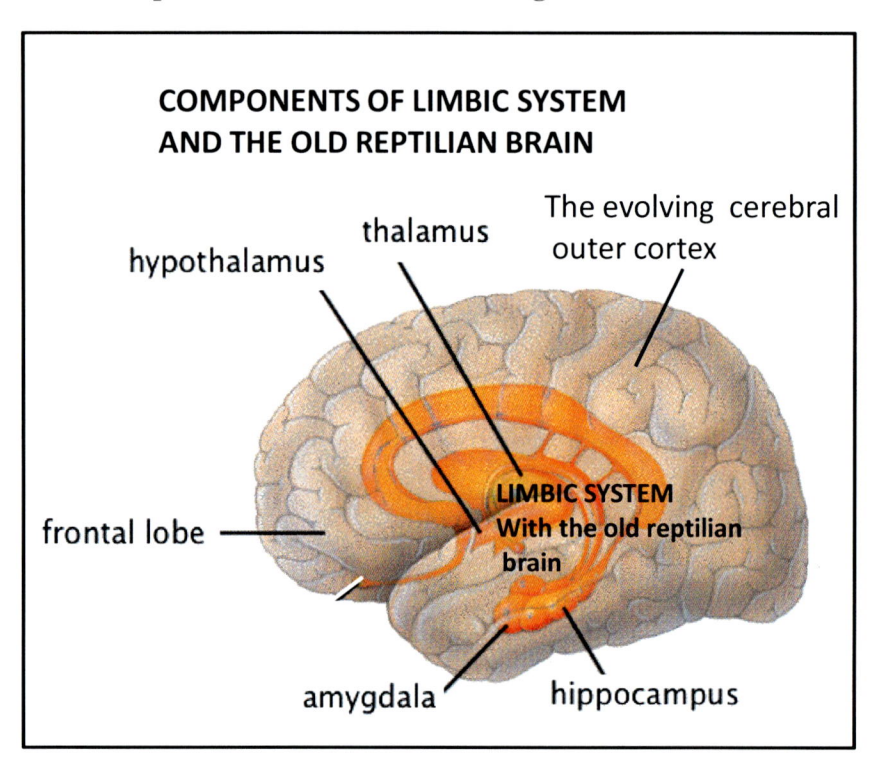

- hypothalamus
- thalamus
- The evolving cerebral outer cortex
- frontal lobe
- LIMBIC SYSTEM With the old reptilian brain
- amygdala
- hippocampus

Figure 28: The Limbic System

It suggested that this limbic system surrounding the reptilian brain area is further subdivided into the cerebellum, which controls balance and coordination; the thalamus, which serves as a kind of switchboard for messages coming from the sensory organs; and the hypothalamus, which regulates the endocrine (or hormonal) activity. The reptilian brain's most familiar function was to set up the bodily functions to 'fight-or-flight' by activating large amounts of the hormone adrenaline to stimulate muscle activity and arousal. (The older reptilian brain area is recently described by Rick Hansen. It confirmed the 'fight-or-flight' response was a functional part of the primitive reptile brain.)

In addition, there was also the amygdala. This was an almond-shaped section of nervous tissue located in the temporal (side) lobe of the brain. It was thought, by some, to be a part of the limbic system, involved with emotional responses. It's possible that signals received from the reptilian brain might be connected to the amygdala and thus influence our emotions and survival instincts. The temporal lobe itself, together with the hippocampus, was involved, together with the neocortex, in retaining longer term memories.

The overlying cerebral cortex comprised the 'grey matter', a network of specially adapted elongated and tentacle-like cells called neurons which could be loosely separated into a 'frontal area', where conscience thinking seemed to be focused. The remaining larger part of the brain cortex, referred to as the neocortex, appeared to deal with the longer-term memory storage and language as shown in Figure 29.

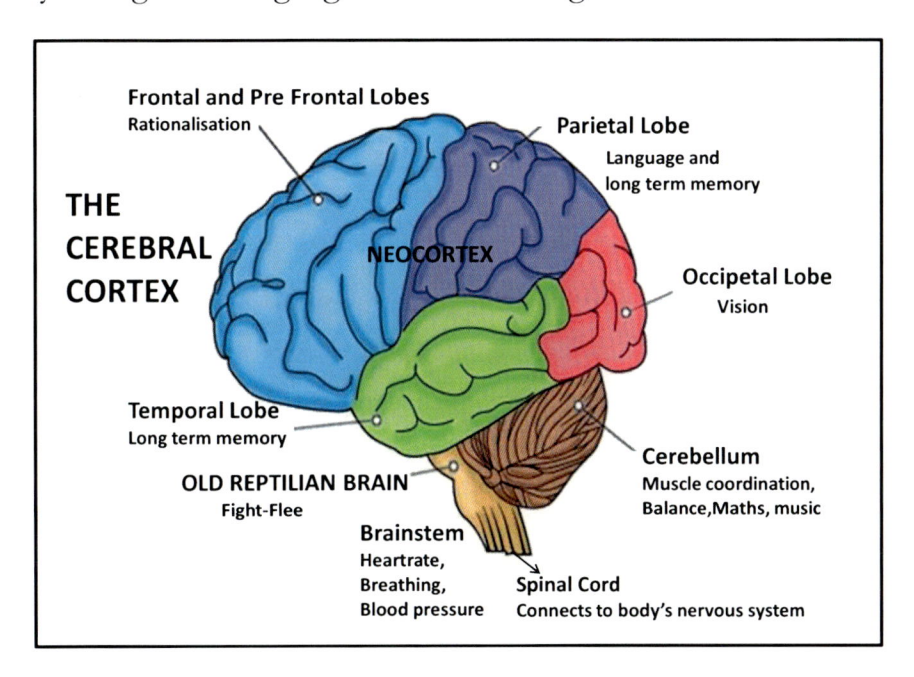

Figure 29: The Cerebral Cortex

Information from the outside world would enter the brain's neural cellular network as pulses known as 'abstraction', as shown in Figure 31. It employs a coding system using variations in the flow of electrons to stimulate variations in the molecular configuration within the neurons. This process is explained with more detail in Figure 31.

Response of a single cell to a bar of light

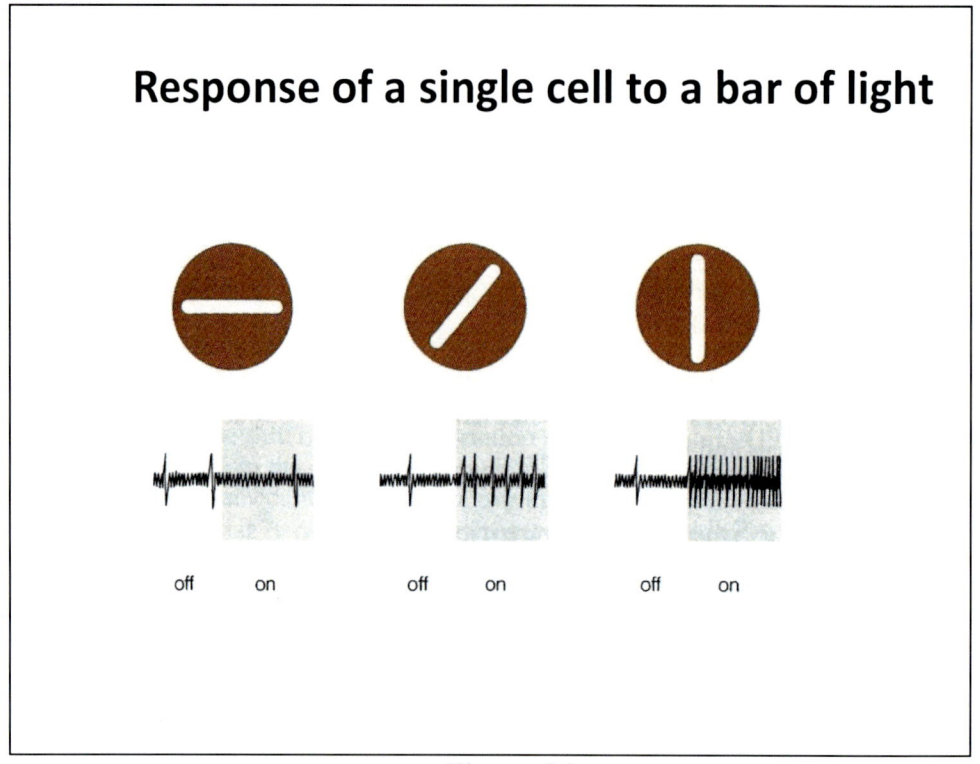

off on   off on   off on

Figure 30

ABSTRACTION PROCESS

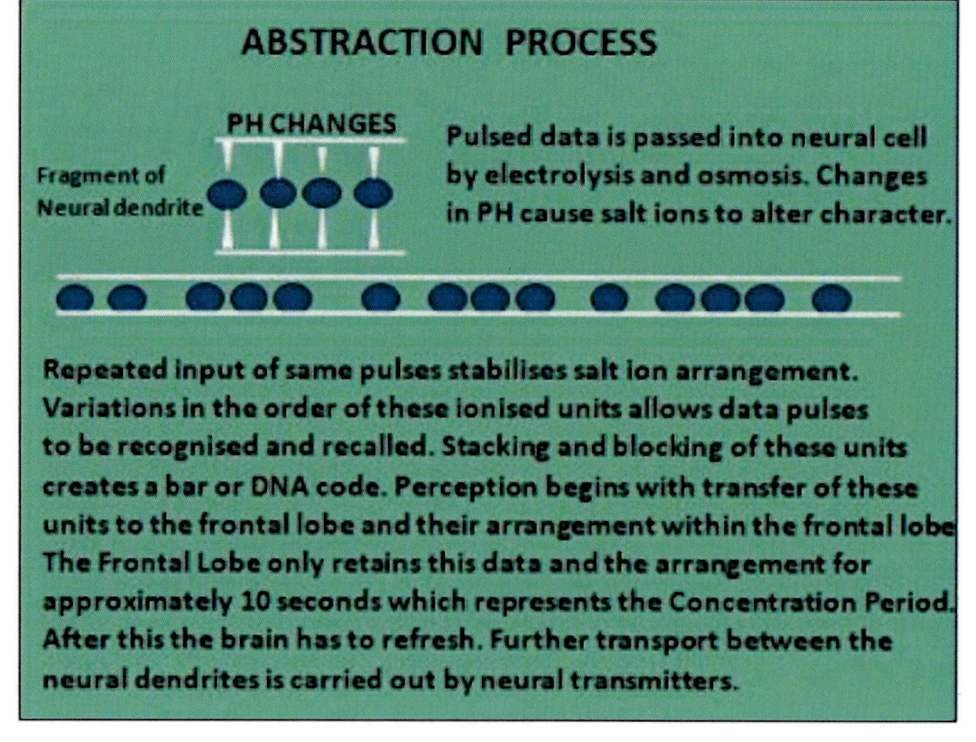

PH CHANGES

Fragment of Neural dendrite

Pulsed data is passed into neural cell by electrolysis and osmosis. Changes in PH cause salt ions to alter character.

Repeated input of same pulses stabilises salt ion arrangement. Variations in the order of these ionised units allows data pulses to be recognised and recalled. Stacking and blocking of these units creates a bar or DNA code. Perception begins with transfer of these units to the frontal lobe and their arrangement within the frontal lobe. The Frontal Lobe only retains this data and the arrangement for approximately 10 seconds which represents the Concentration Period. After this the brain has to refresh. Further transport between the neural dendrites is carried out by neural transmitters.

Figure 31

The result would be a kind of bar code for each tiny piece of information. Figure 30 shows how the electrical signal responds to changes from a single bar of light as it is rotated. The electrical appearance of the pulsed bar code suggested in Figure 31 could be similar and correspond to the changing character of the signals schematically shown in Figure 30.

Obviously enormous volumes of this type of data could be generated and received by the brain. However, this volume could be subsequently reduced (chunked) to speed up later usage of all these tiny details such that a circle or other familiar objects could be instantly recalled. This would mean we only needed to employ a few pieces of data to identify what is going on.

The electrical impulses described above employed an ionised salt solution appeared to be a process not unlike electrolysis. Like a battery, this process would need to recharge after a while, a moment commonly experienced as tiredness. This might be when the old reptilian brain area decides we should sleep.

During our sleep, as the recharging process continues, parts of the previous day's neuron activity might spark activity in the frontal lobe area. We could experience this activity as a dream. Even though this partial data is only random, it's possible the frontal lobe, or elsewhere, would try processing the data rationally just as it would whilst awake. For example, my dream may have included a collage of university, but it could also have a random piece of memory from elsewhere, such as an image of Santa Claus – so he would also enter the dream. In addition, a memory from a visit to the zoo could suddenly introduce a monkey and a lion into the university together with Santa Claus. My brain would try to process and make sense of these new arrivals. The feeling of fear and confusion of this situation would be real since the brain does not realise that it is asleep. As a result, we could wake up feeling frightened and anxious, thinking what a strange dream. Santa Claus was being savaged.

But how did the brain process this data in an intellectual manner? How did it allow us to perceive the outside world and generate new ideas and concepts? Again this process I easily took for granted until I actually asked myself the question. With further thought, I managed to piece together a possible mechanism that could explain this process.

First, it appeared to me that the brain does not take in all the data it could literally see at once. It could only take in at any one time a limited amount of data, so it focuses for a short period on a small area of interest. The sensory organs, eyes, ears, nose and skin would then transfer the full suite of data to the frontal lobe, where it would process a limited part of this volume for about 10 seconds. This is our period of concentration (see Figure 32).

This principle was nicely supported and illustrated by the telephone experiment where most people cannot remember more than about 7 new numbers for more than 10 seconds. After this period, the brain could refresh just like some computer software programs do today. All our concepts and ideas would have to be formulated within these short 10-second periods of concentration. At this time, all the outside data would be imaged and selected, data-coded and sent back into the cortex for recognition and storage together with long-term established memories being brought into the frontal lobe for evaluation with the current data. Each of these periods could be interrupted and refreshed. It must take a lot of work to achieve these concentrated periods. This is probably why it is so irritating to be interrupted whilst trying to concentrate.

Figure 32

Having received this set of data, the brain would begin to interpret it. Three- and four-dimensional spatial relationships are understood from the differences in focal length, sound and time. Other concepts are provided by comparing the present data with concepts already established within the long-term memory. This was best illustrated when the brain has to interpret images in two dimensions alone. The brain does not have the information of depth or time in these pictures, and so, with the help of long-term experience, it offered alternative interpretations of the data. The first drawing could be interpreted as an old woman or a young woman (Figure 33). The painting could include a statue in the foreground or two choirboys in the distance (Figure 34).

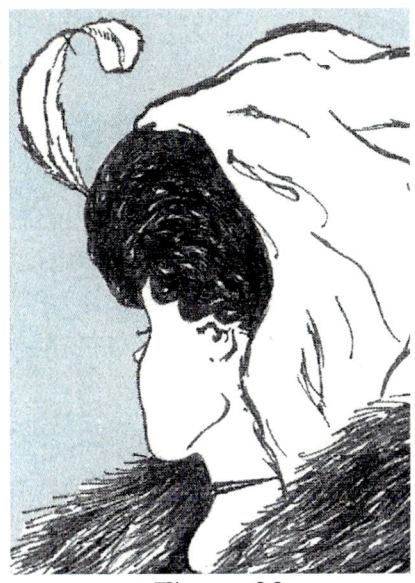

Figure 33   Figure 34

A person's level of perception could be measured to some degree by the ease with which these alternatives could be identified.

The mechanism employed by the brain to internally transfer information from one neuron dendrite to another could employ 'abstraction', as described earlier, and achieved by employing an electro-chemical process employing neurotransmitters. The data would be further transferred around the brain by a suite of molecules referred to as neurotransmitters. When the electrical neural pulse reaches the end of an individual neuron, it would stimulate the neurotransmitters. They act as communicators at the gap between each neuron tentacle (known as the synapse) and enable the transfer of information through a process known as synaptic transmission. So this appears to be how information is transferred around the brain.

There are up to 50 different types of neurotransmitters, many of which are believed to be generated within the amygdala within the inner cerebral cortex. Interestingly, some of them, such as dopamine, serotonin and encephalin, act as natural opiates and are believed to be associated with the generation of pleasure.

PAIN PLEASURE SYNDROME

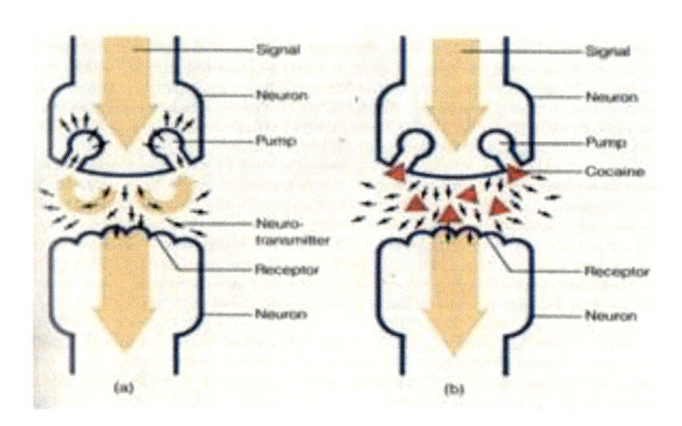

WHEN THE SURVIVAL EQUATION HAS BEEN BALANCED
WE RECEIVE AN APPROPRIATE SUPPLY OF NATURAL OPIATES
WHICH GIVES US THE SENSATION OF PLEASURE AND HAPPINESS.
COCAINE USE CAUSES REDUCTION OF NATURAL OPIATES.

Figure 35

Excess dopamine, for example, could often be associated with euphoria. Encephalin was also associated with giving pleasure, especially in connection with extreme physical exercise. Many commonly used drugs such as Valium and the more dangerous cocaine act on these synaptic junctions the same way. After transmission of the neurotransmitters, some of these molecules would be re-absorbed into the originating neuron while the rest are broken up and made inactive. Cocaine blocks the re-uptake process for neurotransmitters such as the pleasure-producing dopamine (Figure 35). With the re-uptake hampered by cocaine, the normal effects are amplified and the consequent over-abundance of dopamine generates a feeling of euphoria. However, prolonged use of cocaine produces a shortage of these neurotransmitters since the body degrades them at a faster rate than it can manufacture them. With the normal supply depleted by repeated cocaine use, euphoria is replaced by anxiety and depression. This process of uptake and then restriction of opiates such as dopamine I refer to informally as the 'pain-pleasure' syndrome.

These latter descriptions represent the first information and ideas that I could directly employ towards my goal of understanding the controls of happiness. Here, at last, it seems I had found happiness. It was the generation of opiates controlled by the neurotransmitters within the amygdala.

So what else is there to know? Perhaps I could leave the searching at this point, satisfied and content. The reality, however, was that I still knew nothing more about what controlled 'when and where' these neurotransmitters would instigate the opiates under natural conditions. By ingesting drugs, we could artificially initiate pleasure, but 'when and why' does the brain itself naturally initiate pleasure? In other words, I still didn't really understand all the factors that actually controlled happiness.

9

EVOLUTION OF THE BRAIN

Many of my thoughts, at this time, were actively concerned about other college activities. The exam period, for example, tended to focus on the detailed replication of good factual information, and in some ways this was more difficult to achieve. At these times, I had to deviate my attention away from 'idle thoughts' about the brain and get on with some serious revision. It required significant devotion to repetition and recitation, an area I was not suited to. I could amble around pathways and roads for miles dreaming about the philosophy and mechanisms, but if you asked me for lists of names, then I was lost. My thoughts were unordered, and really only taking into consideration information that I thought might help me explain the function of happiness. I seemed to be quite absent in other areas. In addition, I suffered from a long period of illness that prevented me from taking any exams in my second year. So in the mainstream of academia, I was not making good progress.

Like many other students of human behaviour, I was a devoted people watcher and derived an abundant supply of data from the simple observation of friends and other students around me. From time to time, a lunchtime conversation at college would include a sprinkling of ideas with regard to this part of philosophical science. Martin, in particular, was similarly interested in how different people reacted to various types of everyday situations.

One particular day, as I steered my way to the college canteen, such thoughts were still bubbling in my mind. The menu was limited. It was a choice of a leathery egg or dried, hard-baked chili con carne. I chose the egg together with the ubiquitous supply of baked beans. As I sat down and began to eat, I found myself looking around the hall. Although it was a refectory, it doubled as a dancehall at weekends, and because it was so large, for some it was also a place to study. It had a high ceiling, and the sound of voices tended to merge into a general hum. That day, however, it was relatively empty. Giles, a charismatic figure in the university, was holding forth on an adjacent table. Two of his disciples listened intently as he gestured authoritatively. He was a master of the spoken language, smooth and dangerous but fascinating. Able to reduce his fellow students to whimpering fools by his cool, ruthless and manipulative oratory. Strangely it was just the type that was likely to suffer most – those who were drawn into his counselling. If Charles Manson had a brother, it was Giles. Briefly, as his gaze was directed towards my table, I felt threatened and immediately looked back to the relative safety of my own table. Nevertheless, I was always fascinated with this character and tried to eavesdrop on their conversation. It wasn't to be. Suddenly the hush in the hall was broken. Below is a typical example of our conversations.

'Why is this guy sitting all on his own, then?' said an almost shrill, but comic, voice from behind. 'He looks *so* bored!'

I recognised the voice. It was Martin and another colleague from our geology year named Graham.

'Well, we're going to change all this, aren't we, 'cos we're going to sit here as well,' said Martin, continuing the performance.

'Yep, it's too late now 'cos we're here now,' followed Graham in an equally animated tone.

Rory, another student geologist also joined them as they deliberately continued the fuss of sitting down. I caught a glimpse of Giles as he turned his head away in semi-disdain at the intrusion of this noise. It mattered not; I was very pleased to see them. Their humour was instant and fun – even if at times mockingly infantile.

'There's no need to sulk, you know,' began Martin again, 'is there, Rory?'

'No need to sulk at all,' confirmed Rory in a similar but softer tone.

'Why doesn't he need to sulk?' interceded Graham as he stared at the unusual colour of the minced meat in his shepherd's pie. This type of nonsense conversation was just a form of greeting for Martin. He continued.

'Well, I've just seen Gallosher Dunlop,' he said, using his affectionate name for one of our lecturers called Dr Dunlop. 'And she says the Cheese and Wine Seminar is tomorrow and not to forget . . . and be sure to tell that Mike not to sulk.' The wine and cheeses at the seminar were supposed to be a part of our general education in the more refined areas of entertaining.

'Why should I sulk, Martin, when there are guys like you around to cheer me up?' I weakly retorted, finally able to find space. 'I've obviously nothing to worry about.' I added, this time with a mock smile.

Martin feigned offence. 'Words, Michael. They're merely words.' And then, without pause, he said, 'Incidentally I have one word for you.'

'And that is?' I asked expectantly.

'Fred Hoyle,' he said proudly, clearly using two words, but I wasn't about to rise to that. 'I went to hear him talk at UC yesterday evening and he's got something. He talks about the cosmos, space travel and everything.'

'With a name like that, he doesn't sound very cosmic,' I said unbelievingly.

'Cosmic, man,' said Graham flatly as he watched a bright yellow stain of custard run down the front of his bright red jumper.

'It was all about the origin of life and it began, not here on earth but out there in the galaxy somewhere, millions of years before it arrived here on earth,' said Martin emphatically.

Graham continued to stare down at the changing pattern on his jumper as he vacantly debated whether to lick the custard off directly.

Martin continued, trying to ignore the antics of Graham, 'Everything evolved from the hydrogen atom by the nuclear reactions which took place within the interior of stars. Thus everything that happened at an atomic level was established during the early development of the solar

systems. Not here on earth as you suggested, Mike.'
'Amen,' said Rory.

'It was thought molecular construction was still primarily an earthly affair. However' – Martin paused momentarily – 'and this is the interesting part' – he paused again – 'the basic molecules required for the construction of organic matter have been found in meteorites. They are rich in organic chemicals.'

Martin's eyes seemed to glow as he gazed towards an imaginary meteorite. He continued to hold our attention despite the urgent attention required to Graham's jumper.

I liked what he said. It seemed to overcome a lot of the chance required in the previous ideas for generating the first organic particles which were heavily reliant on chance combinations of atoms and fortuitous lightning for energy.

'Thus, the origin of organic molecules, the building blocks for life, were already prefabricated in other parts of the galaxy,' I said thoughtfully.

'How convenient,' said Graham, with a faint edge of sarcasm.

'It could even be that the some of these molecules had evolved further, even as far as DNA and the first cell,' exclaimed Martin.

'Even more convenient,' said Rory, echoing Graham's previous hint of sarcasm.

It looked like Martin was not going to continue.

'What is it with you two?' I suddenly blurted out. 'This is interesting . . . isn't it?' I was becoming very aware of their growing boredom.

'Nope!' came the instant reply.

Both Graham and Rory shook their heads emphatically. They were ready to move on. To make their point, they both stood up noisily and pointed in the general direction of the bar. Giles turned and scornfully scrutinised why the peace of the refectory had been shattered yet again. As we walked along the corridor, Martin finished off his story.

Certainly Martin's visit to the lecture at UC was very timely. It seemed to clarify so much about the beginnings of life. And yet it took nothing away from my developing thoughts concerning the links between human, cellular, molecular and atomic behavioural patterns. I was convinced that all our behaviour, even our most reverent of thoughts or emotions, was only physics in action, a simple equation of mass and energy being forced to establish a correct balance and then trying to sustain it. That's what controls our behaviour.

I passed some of these thoughts onto Martin, who immediately added that behaviour was simply a prelude to sex. He said it as a joke, but somehow it had a ring of truth about it. In fact, this last comment attracted the interest of Graham.

'What do you think of my behaviour, Martin?' he asked, raising an arm and conspicuously scratching his armpit.

'It's abysmal' came the immediate response.

'Does that mean you won't have sex with me?' said Graham indignantly.

'That's right,' replied Martin without expression.

'Really, you won't?' said Graham yet again.

'Nope, I'm sorry but I will not have sex with you.' Martin's voice had taken on a fatherly tone.

'If I promise to behave myself?' came the enquiry again.

'Well you'd have to improve a lot,' said Martin, appearing to yield a little.

'Then will you take me to the dance?' said Graham, pointing to a poster on the corridor wall. 'Please, please!'

They proceeded down the corridor with the continuing sound of this most eccentric of conversations. Rory and I stared at each other with a bemused look.

'Talking of which,' I followed, 'are you going to the dance?'

Rory looked shocked. 'I hope you're not asking me to take you,' he said, taking a step back.

'I'll take that as a no, then.'

As I continued along the corridor, my thoughts returned to the discoveries of Fred Hoyle. It was very interesting that the basic building blocks for life could be found in outer space. It turned my thinking upside down. Despite the intriguing nature of this thought, I will deal with the consequences a little later. My attention, for the time being, was still focused on the nature of the brain. The target was still to find a convincing mechanism to control happiness.

Unfortunately, no book I had encountered at this time attempted to provide a fully integrated model of brain functions and how all the different parts fit together to control our feelings, emotions and behaviour. There was an abundance of factual information relating to the detail of the biochemical and physical processes going on within the brain but very little explaining the connection to the more everyday but important emotions that we all regularly experience. They described substances that could generate the sensation of happiness but still not the dynamics of why we feel happy, what function it served and why it is so difficult to sustain. Clearly somewhere in the layout and arrangement of the upper cerebral cortex and lower limbic system lay the answer. So in which parts of the brain should I focus?

Simply stated, I decided to focus on the frontal cortex, temporal lobe and limbic system.

The cerebral cortex clearly affected our behaviour and must have eventually affected, in some way, our happiness, but with the evidence in front of me, I just couldn't see how. I would toy with theoretical models, explore more avenues about synaptic activities, but at that time I couldn't find the answer I was after.

My progress would have ended there if I hadn't by chance read a short account of some experimentation carried out on the old reptilian brain complex. It was only a few lines, but it was enough to catch my attention and to start me thinking. During the experiment, they had discovered that mild electrical stimulation of certain areas in the old reptilian complex produces feelings of pleasure whilst stimulation of adjacent regions produces sensations that are unpleasant or painful. Such observation lent support to a concept that anxiety and even happiness might in some way be controlled from this old reptilian complex. Perhaps the old reptilian brain originally controlled the 'fight-or-flight' response but was linked with the amygdala to generate the pleasure or pain requirement. It began to point towards an important link between the frontal lobe activities and the old reptilian complex (Figures 28 and 29).

Presumably our thought processes within the frontal cortex were connected to this process and in some way initiated this activity. An interesting thought – but did this primitive structure really receive and process the complex perceptions of the cerebral cortex? And if so, how?

I began a closer look at the nature of the so-called reptilian brain and its evolution into mammals. It appeared mammals evolved from a group of reptiles called the synapsids. Although mammals came into their own only after the extinction of the dinosaurs some 65 million years ago, mammals had maintained a low-profile existence for some 150 million years before that. Since the original writing of this text, there have been new fossil discoveries that reveal more of this early history. Recently, in 2001, researchers reported that a fossil found in China in 1985 was the remains of a tiny, furry animal that was a relative of the living mammals today but lived 195 million years ago in the Early Jurassic period. Called *Hadrocodium wui*, the little creature had certain key mammalian features 40 million years earlier than had previously been known from the fossil record (ref. Michael Novacek).

Descended from more archaic reptilian relatives, the early true mammals were mainly small insect-eating creatures adapted to night-time activity.

They ranged in size from scarcely bigger than a bumblebee to squirrel-sized, keeping out of the way of the predatory dinosaurs. They acquired certain traits that would characterise mammals afterwards: limbs positioned under the body, a more complex physiology, milk-producing glands, and a diverse array of teeth, which included incisors, canines, premolars, molars and, most importantly, an 'enlarged brain'. Presumably this enlargement included an evolving cerebral cortex.

In the early Cainozoic era, after the dinosaurs became extinct, the number and diversity of mammals seems to have exploded. In just 10 million years (a brief time by geologic standards) about 130 genera (groups of related species) had evolved, encompassing some 4,000 species. These included the first fully aquatic mammals (whales) and flying mammals (bats), as well as rodents and, most importantly, primates. The first primate-like mammals, or proto-primates, evolved in the early Palaeocene epoch (65.5–55.8 million years ago) at the beginning of the Cainozoic era. They were roughly similar to squirrels and tree shrews in size and appearance. The existing, very fragmentary fossil evidence (from Asia, Europe, North Africa and especially Western North America) suggests that they were adapted to an arboreal way of life. They probably were equipped with relatively good eyesight as well as hands and feet adapted for climbing in trees. Such activities would demand a larger cortex to cope with the precise decision-making required. However, the reptilian brain complex with the 'fight-or-flight' response was still the most important survival structure and thus would probably have been preserved and integrated in an area below the evolving cerebral cortex, together with a primitive limbic system.

Humans and the great apes (large apes) of Africa, chimpanzees and gorillas, share a common ancestor that lived between 8 and 6 million years ago – *Orrorin tugenensis*, the oldest human ancestor thought to have walked on two legs. During this time, it seems likely additional layers of the evolving and developing cerebral cortex continued to be added. Nevertheless, its primary survival function, the original 'fight-or-flight' mechanism, was always preserved and integrated.

This was obviously a very important survival process, and even whilst there were evolving connections to the frontal lobe, it would appear during extreme threatening situations, the reptilian brain would return to its old original function and directly process incoming sensory data without passing through the slower channel of the frontal lobe of the cerebral cortex. We could now decide subconsciously, in a matter of a micro-second, whether we were going to fight-or-flight.

Let's take, for example, the simple situation where you are walking along the road. All is proceeding well until at a certain moment you become aware of a dark area in front of you which you are about to step on. At the last second you realise that this dark area is, in fact, a big hole in the road created by the absence of a manhole cover. The step you are taking is going to send you cascading down into the hole. At almost this same moment, the 'fight-or-flight' mechanism takes over and sets in motion a whole series of actions within the body's metabolism which allows the coordination of limbs sufficiently fast to save you from the fateful fall, a welcome conclusion to the story.

The story served to illustrate how rapidly the complex of information is relayed from the observation to the instant of recovery. Dangerous situations, like our example, described above, needed an extremely fast reaction time, and it would seem reasonable to consider the old reptilian brain would take raw data directly from the sensory organs in these situations.

Instinctively, the idea that massive amounts of data involving complex situations with details of sight, smell, sound and others being received by the newly evolved cerebral cortex and then sent to this lowly primitive reptilian brain seemed unreasonable. In other words, I felt it more reasonable that the genetic code of DNA had evolved cells within the frontal lobe of the cerebral cortex to assess and interpret the incoming sensory data so that only the essential data was transmitted to the old reptilian brain. This way, DNA could receive a danger signal more rapidly and, in effect, directly influence its own survival.

Despite the clear ability of this reptilian part of the brain to act independently and be capable of producing pleasurable opiates, I had no actual evidence that its ability to stimulate pain and pleasure was connected to the cerebral cortex and its complex processes. My question concerning happiness still remained unanswered. But perhaps I was asking the wrong question. Maybe I should ask, 'Why would the more advanced highly developed cerebral cortex, with all its abilities of perception and intellect, wish to surrender its more sophisticated information back down to the old, more primitive reptilian brain complex?'

The simple answer was of course 'survival' and, in particular, survival of DNA. As the cerebral cortex began to evolve over and around the original reptilian brain, it took sensory data from the frontal lobe and sent signals to the old reptilian complex. This way, DNA would have been able to improve the ability to assess the outside world for danger or threatening circumstances. The additional data from the early newly surrounding cerebral cortex may have been relatively small.

At this time, our brain must have been similar to that of the small mammals we have today although present-day small mammals may have more cerebral cortex and a more advanced limbic system than their primitive predecessors. Since there would have been a minimal frontal lobe or intelligent thought mechanisms in place, the activity of mammals at this early stage would have been primarily automotive and thus most likely subconscious. Just like our own experience when we almost fall, there is no emotion at the instant of correcting the fall. Thus, life for the primitive mammals, without the addition of a large cerebral cortex, may have been largely automotive with very little awareness of its own actions and the consequences of its actions.

As the cerebral cortex developed further within the human and the signals became more voluminous and complex, it also seemed reasonable to speculate that the entire cerebral data set could have been compacted and simplified to save valuable survival time. This type of compaction has already been discussed, observed at infancy to save well-known objects such as a circle being fully described again. A part of the evolving cortex, at this time, may have been set aside to sort the incoming data, find out what was important and thus reduce the volume for the old reptilian complex to deal with. This could be considered the beginning of consciousness and reason. So instead of all the incoming data arriving at once, only the essential survival data from the outer cortex (probably within the frontal cortex) was sent down to the old reptilian brain complex. The rest was now stored for later use, in the temporal lobe initiating our long-term memory. The process became part of a tripartite system, which I discuss in more detail in the next section. The fact that most of the neurotransmitters were generated within the amygdala also supports the idea that a great volume of data received by the frontal lobe would be chunked or compressed (similar to today's computer ZIP file) prior to sending to the old reptilian brain. This would have enabled a more rapid transmission to the old reptilian brain to initiate 'fight-or-flight', vital for survival. Perhaps only then, after the information is relayed on to the amygdala, is the ZIP file decompressed and the full context of the interpreted data set assessed for dopamine delivery.

Since I began writing this story, supporting evidence for the above concept has recently been suggested. It concludes that the frontal lobe is involved in conscious thought and higher mental functions, particularly in that part of the frontal lobe now known as the prefrontal cortex (Figure 36). In addition, it has been proposed that the inherited old reptilian complex could already instigate adrenaline to initiate 'fight-or-flight', together with some degree of opiate (dopamine) production (Lovell et al., 2015). However, it seemed likely that some level of opiate control must have also been conducted by the amygdala.

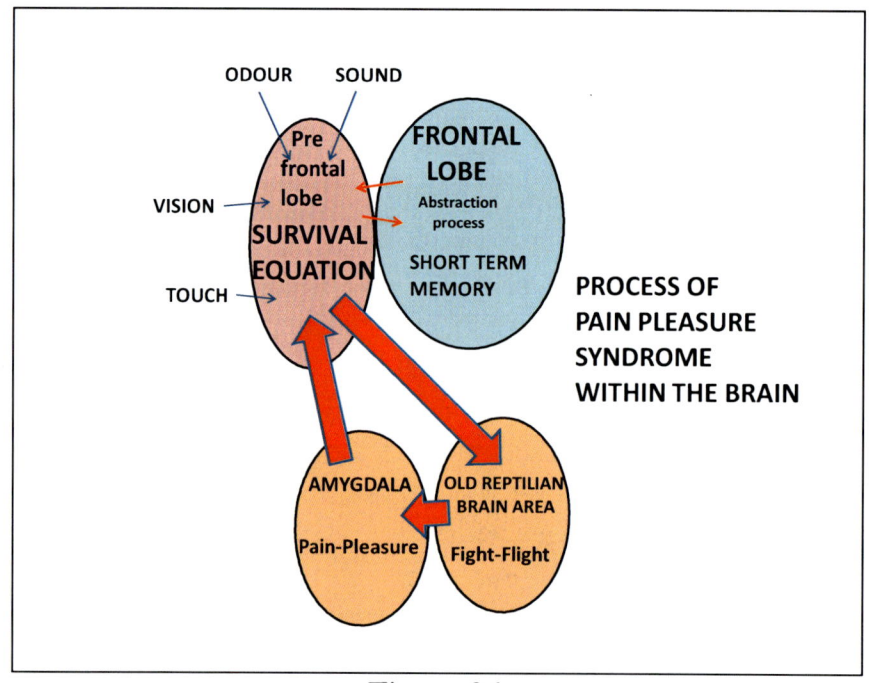

Figure 36

The previous direct and subconscious method of data flow involving the old reptilian brain, however, may have still continued on a more limited basis. There is no reason to suppose it stopped entirely since it offers the primary survival mechanism. For example, the reptilian brain could cross-check the summarised information sent down from the frontal lobe by accessing via its old direct route. I will show how I continued to explore this concept and its consequences a little later.

For a moment I would like to speculate further about the compression mechanism and my proposed idea that each situation could be summarised within the evolving frontal lobe of the cerebral cortex prior to sending down to the old reptilian brain complex. It seemed reasonable to suppose that this summarised and compressed message indicated the 'severity of danger and security' since this is the essential information required by the DNA of the old reptilian brain. For convenience, I assumed the 'severity of danger and security' to be indicated by a simple score of 1:10, perhaps related to the strength and character of the emitted signal. The scale of this score could be assessed by the reptilian brain, which then decided how much anxiety or pleasure the situation demanded (see Figure 36). The result could be then passed on to the amygdala, which opens the compressed message.

The interesting point in this hypothesis is not the detail of the 'fight-or-flight' mechanism itself but the possible principle of the brain's immensely complex thought processes being simplified and compressed into a simple score and then this triggering a major reaction within the body.

But why did the body wish to translate our more subtle observations and thoughts into pain and pleasure? Why would it wish to do this? I could understand the need to readjust our fall into a hole, but how does, for example, the happiness of listening to a piece of music or doing a crossword puzzle help our survival?

To explain this, I first considered the nature of the data set formulated within the cerebral cortex. Earlier I established that everything we do is directed towards our survival and that of our offspring. With the consequent transfer of DNA via a suitable partner to the offspring, the security of future generations is assured. This being the case, it stands to reason that the sole occupation of the brain is towards these objectives – that every single observation and subsequent thought process is concerned entirely with the survival of your particular DNA.

Perhaps this thought process and survival assessment within the prefrontal lobe could be envisaged as a 'survival equation'.

10

THE SURVIVAL EQUATION

So what is this 'survival equation' and how does it work? Well, it seems fairly obvious. The simplest survival equation was drawn on a cave wall thousands of years ago as represented in the primitive cave drawing shown in Figure 37.

PICTURE SHOWS ANIMALS BEING HUNTED AND SPEARED

Figure 37

The father shows his son the picture of the buffalo and hunter with a bow and arrow. Finally, there is a picture of a buffalo dead on the ground with arrows in it and people are feeding off it. When the boy reads these pictures, he would receive a dose of pleasure because this sequence is actually a survival equation. He realises that the problem of hunger can be resolved by hunting to achieve the solution of food. In effect, a survival equation could be simply:-

> **Problem (Hunger) + Resolution (Hunting)
> = Solution (Food and Survival)**

The solution would then be given a survival score, and we would receive an appropriate amount of dopamine for the idea, which then encourages us to continue. Once viewed this way, I realised that everything we do could be a survival equation. Even our most abstract activities could be enactments of survival equations as was the boy looking at the picture on the cave wall.

Abstract activities
Let's look at some of these abstract activities I considered.

Science
For example, mathematics is as old as the caveman. The problem '1 buffalo + 1 buffalo = 2 buffalo (twice as much food)' receives a high survival score. Mathematics therefore has tremendous survival value.

Science is a similar story. A scientific experiment sets up a problem which we try to resolve. As scientists begin to see the way forward and as a solution looks likely, a feeling of pleasure and excitement begins to take over, encouraging them to continue with this activity, as suggested in Figures 36 and 38.

Figure 38

This is because the solution to this problem is likely to increase DNA's security. As the final conclusion is reached and the 'anticipated' successful result is confirmed, the final dose of pleasure (dopamine) is ended. He will get not get this same level of pleasure again if he repeats the same experiment because DNA already has knowledge of this newfound security. And since the experiment yields no extra security, there is no extra pleasure and so it becomes boring to continue. This way, a scientist will be motivated to think of an entirely new experiment to get the pleasure again and thus takes his first fatal step towards being a workaholic.

Humour

It appears to be a similar process for the 'joke'. We are given a circumstance which suggests a predictable outcome. For example, I could tell you that 'once upon a time there were two fishes in a tank'. This information is passed down as offering little new additional survival value. Nothing new is being offered, so there is no change in the dopamine levels. In fact, you, as the audience, has a certain expectancy now of any future answers and is almost getting ready to yawn. Your intense focus on this tank is not very interesting. Then I continue and add that one of the fishes says to the other,

'Can you drive this thing? Because I can't'.

After hearing this, it's possible you laugh 'ha ha' or smile (or perhaps you don't).

Figure 39

Your brain has in fact conducted a kind of scientific investigation of the first sentence and then repeated this investigation again with the addition of new information. In doing this process, it has discovered an entirely new interpretation with all kinds of connotations. The brain raises the level of your dopamine to encourage you to investigate these. As the brain continues the processing, it resolves the equation into at least three different ways, rewarding each investigation with some dopamine as you process the equation.

1. The first is that the tank is a normal glass fish tank filled with water.

2. The second is that the fish are actually inside an armoured gun tank.

3. The third is the possibility that these fish could actually drive the tank and can be envisaged running amok within the battlefield.

The processing is often repeated, adding to the pleasure, because the brain checks and rechecks to be sure these interpretations are correct. DNA needs to reassure itself. It needs to know how each particular scenario affects its security. We can do this immediately by stepping outside this imagined reality of the 'joke' and releasing ourselves from the situation. But since the process usually carries the element of discovery and is thus rewarded with dopamine, most of us continue. The more structurally correct and believable the joke is, the more this process continues and the more pleasure you receive until the brain is finally convinced which interpretation is correct, and there is no need to recheck. If the joke is retold again, it has no effect. The survival value of the processed equations are all known. The laugh may be a consequence of temporarily holding your breath during repeated concentration periods whilst your brain assesses and re-assesses the circumstance. Once the joke is realised, you exhale rapidly, making the sound of a laugh.

Art
The abstract world of art is yet again a survival equation which began with the diagram of the buffalo on the cave wall discussed above. Clearly pictures and other abstract objects carry messages within their structure and arrangement which can communicate security to DNA. When this happens, we feel the pleasure of the dopamine sent by the old reptilian brain complex for the process of realising this message of security. So what kind of security is offered by a picture?

Well, the diagrammatic picture of the buffalo is obvious and has already been explained. Some of the most popular pictures are the impressionist paintings from the latter part of the 19th century and the early 20th. These are modified representations of the countryside, villages and rivers with people in everyday situations. The artist employs several techniques of layout, colour and detail to provide the observer with security. The layout often shows a road or river leading into the picture and leading to an horizon or turning a corner. The observer's eye is led along this road and to the horizon, which creates a feeling of continuation and things to come. In other words, the picture points to a future. This is a message DNA likes to receive. It likes to see there might be something just around the corner. At the same time, the horizon or corner is placed at the ratio of approximately one-third to two-thirds of the picture area. This represents a universal ratio inherent in all organic life. Leonardo da Vinci discovered this more precisely as 1:1.6 whilst studying art and biology. It became known as the Golden Mean. Organic structures appear to function at their optimum when they are placed adjacent to each other in these proportions. As a consequence, the face of a human contains a great number of these ratios within the features, which enable it to demonstrate it is healthy to a potential partner. Such features we consider desirable and refer to them as beautiful (Figure 40).

Paintings of beautiful faces are consequently very popular since they automatically convey a lot of pleasure. The artist continues this principle into its paintings if he wants to communicate a message of peace and beauty. The horizon or corner arranged in these ratios already gives us a comforting feeling. By making the picture abstract and not literal, the artist has depersonalised the scene with less detail. This takes away any reference to a specific person or habitat and as a result removes the competitive and unpleasant elements of life. This makes the picture more relaxing and available to the observer and allows everyone to make the picture their own. The colours and textures can be adjusted from reality to suggest calm or perhaps lively atmosphere by their strength and brightness. The observer detects all these features and is consequently drawn to the picture (Figure 41).

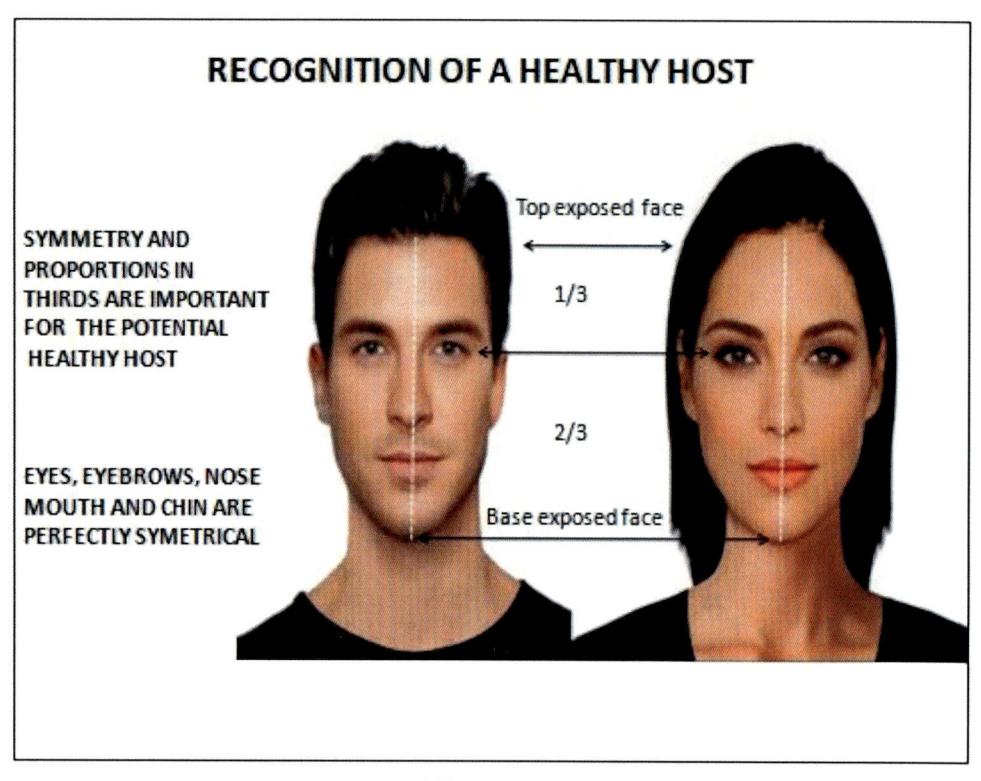

Figure 40

Figure 41

Pictures can easily be reduced to symbolic representations of these same reassuring objects. So long as the proportions and textures are maintained, the observer can still feel a calm message coming through. That is why artists often start their career with detail and end it with merely symbolic representations of more or less the same thing. They realised it provided the same amount of pleasure.

However, not all pictures are designed to send a message of calm. Some artists wish to express their horror or discomfort with life. By distorting the above ratios, textures and colours, a disturbing message of disharmony and discomfort can be received by the observer.

Fiction
A story in book or film form is a very obvious survival equation. As we concentrate on the story, we shut out reality and only process the incoming data from the page of the book or the dialogue of the film. Take for example a story about a man who has been robbed. The brain sends down the information that the possibility exists that savings can be stolen. Your frontal lobe is able to 'visualise' the awful consequences and that your security could be threatened. This information is given a low survival score and relayed down to the old reptilian brain. The resulting restriction of dopamine and increase of adrenalin makes you feel uncomfortable, even stressed. Your DNA feels insecure. As a consequence, you have a strong urge to read on to find a resolution. Fortunately, into the story arrives a clever detective, who resolves the problem and discovers where the money is located. The savings are finally recovered. Provided you are still only focused on the story, your body receives a wave of pleasure. This wave of pleasure is gratefully received, which then urges you to read another detective book.

Hollywood films often concentrate on the storyline that yields the highest dopamine rush, that is, the survival of the family and, in particular, a successful future for the children. A typical storyline begins with the scene of a family happily playing together in the garden of their home. But then the family is threatened, the children are brutally abducted and the distraught parents are thrown into panic and frantically embark on a subsequent search. There are hints that the children are in mortal danger, and it is only a matter of time before they may perish. During this period, whilst all other reality is shut out, we feel anxious and uncomfortable. We continue to watch in hopes that the problem will be resolved. Suddenly the situation looks bleak, as a message is relayed that a body in the neighbouring town has been reportedly found. The feeling of discomfort that can arise within us, by our ability to visualise the consequences of these threatening situations, can turn to distress This would be especially true in those of us who are parents since your DNA via the tripartite system would feel threatened, fearing that its own host could lose a child. Fortunately, all usually ends happily as the children are found safe and well. The final scene of the family all back together, playing in the garden again, the children returned, reassures our DNA all is well again and secure. At the realisation of this moment, we are sent a wave of dopamine and we are very happy that we watched the film to the end.

Even the most distorted and violent storylines can include this theme in the background. The final scene of a movie may show a fearless hunter, clothes torn and bloodstained, after fighting a lion. The hunter holding a rifle in the one hand and a child he has just saved from certain death in the other. So long as we see this as the conclusion, our DNA can be pleased with the outcome, and we are able to still experience some pleasure despite the displayed violence.

Music

Music works on many levels but is in fact a form of mathematics in sound. The sonic signature of sound is three-dimensional. It looks a little like an elongated bubble of oil within one of those ornamental lamps or light displays. Within two dimensions we can detect if the primary note relates to the musical frequency of C or D, and so on. The spatial arrangement of the primary notes within the initial theme sets up the problem, that is, the sonic frequencies, both single and multiple harmonic note associations. The variations of these spatial relationships that follow have to mathematically relate to the spatial problem set by the initial theme. If this is resolved properly and a safe return to the initial theme is achieved, then the brain perceives this as having survival value, and so we receive a wave of pleasure. The third dimension to the sound of the primary note is tonal quality. This carries information relating to character of the sound. Human, animal and inanimate sounds of nature can be imitated and added into this third dimension, which gives the final quality to the note. The listener can then detect qualities within the music, such as sweet, coarse, rasping and others. With imagination, this combination of note and tone can be made to imitate the sound of anger, the roar of the sea, the coarse cry of an animal, the soothing tone of a loved one. Add to this a positive storyline within the lyrics, then the pleasure is doubly enhanced. Add to this a rhythm that is simulating that of sexual arousal, then the effect gets stronger. Repeating the inherent survival equation within the musical structure and you get repeat after repeat of dopamine. Such music can lead eventually to an ecstatic trance.

In more detail, the effects of the music on your emotions could possibly be explained as follows. Let's take for example a simple nursery rhyme tune, *Mary Had a Little Lamb*. If the tune is played in a Major key with even spacing and emphasis on the regular tone of the notes, the effect is predictable, especially if the music finishes on the key note (the same note on which it started). The brain finds the tune easy and predictable to follow, with all notes following in a reassuringly regular and expected manner and safely returning to the original note it started on. The brain perceives no indication for concern (Figure 42).

Figure 42

If we reduce the interval of one of the notes, a strong harmonic third, we hear this as a change from a Major to a minor key (Figure 43).

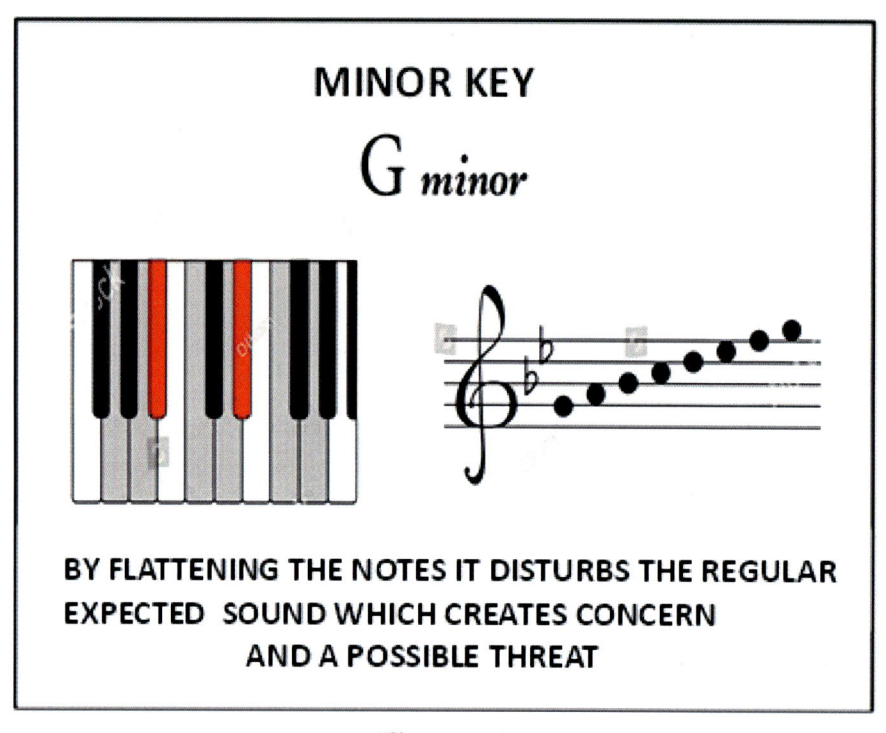

MINOR KEY

G *minor*

BY FLATTENING THE NOTES IT DISTURBS THE REGULAR EXPECTED SOUND WHICH CREATES CONCERN AND A POSSIBLE THREAT

Figure 43

The tune does not hit the expected note but one that is diminished 'flattened'. It may also come in sooner than expected followed by the next note that is consequently delayed. This is recognised by the brain as uncertainty and a possible error, which is disturbing. The lack of predictability is interpreted as a potential threat and sets up a tension within you. Such music is often used to support films trying to show danger and menace. The more notes we diminish, the more tension and disturbance it generates within the mind until the music sounds like a cacophony. Add to this a change in the lyrics such as 'Mary had a giant snake' and the tension increases.

Jazz music uses this disturbing effect to challenge. Very often, the melody begins in the Major key, with the predictable sequence of a popular and well-known melody. But jazz musicians never like to stick to the predictable and thus begin to diminish the melody by degrees but in such a way that it still supports the mathematical frame work of a balanced tune. The final sequence almost always returns you safely back to the original predictable melody. This way, the carefully listening brain gets the double bonus of satisfying two inherent survival equations: one which was the predictable tune and the other diminished version. The latter version also carried a threat of uncertainty, which was resolved as you were led home to the main theme. Listening to jazz can be very satisfying so long as the ear is allowed to take in all the notes and follow the equation carefully to its completion. Jazz music requires concentration and is sometimes mistaken as a moment to socialise where the listener is distracted by ongoing conversation during the performance. The full equation cannot be heard, and consequently the unconnected fragments of diminished notation become irritating to the listener. It's not surprising that this style of music attracts a specialised and limited audience.

One more example from the music world can be illustrated by the music of the classical composer Mahler in his *5th Symphony*. During his career, the composer must have experienced loss and the yearning that can bring. This inner feeling must have been inconsolable. Mahler, however, was able to express this loss and the longing for something that he knew could never be in his music. He used switches from minor to Major and other subtle diminished harmonics in a majestic way to reflect the disturbed but powerful feelings within. In addition, however, he also added the almost agonising effect of creating a beautifully balanced theme poised to land safely back to the pleasurable rewards of the final keynote and then deliberately avoiding this note by climbing back into the theme a little longer. He sometimes repeated this two or three times and, by doing so, created a feeling intense longing within the listener whose DNA by now was yearning for the reassuring message that the home key note had been reached. The absence of this note only increases the yearning. This is why I believe his *5th Symphony* is such a powerful piece of music.

The eventual arrival of the key note momentarily gives the theme a happy ending, a moment when he can be reunited with the happiness felt before. This was utilised beautifully in the theme music from the film *Death in Venice*.

By contrast, the Beatles were famous for the optimism, warmth and excitement they created in their music. They frequently employed the predictable nature of the Major key as a basis. But instead of creating uncertainty by way of diminishing the spatial intervals, they enhanced and reaffirmed the cheerful news that all is well by repeating the same phrase as a series of climbing crescendos within several related but completely different Major keys. If we consider the impact of their first significant worldwide hit, it begins with the famous phrase 'she loves you yeah, yeah, yeah'. As we have discussed earlier, these words already state a very positive and exciting bit of news. This is the most exciting news that the DNA can wish to hear (as we will discuss more fully a little later). Add to this a rising series of notes with wonderfully reassuring spacing, climbing higher by their clever innuendo that they are changing key without actually doing so the excitement is increased. The first phrase is sung with E minor, the second with the harmonically related A major as though the whole melody is going to shift into the key of A. Instead, the third phrase is sang with the harmonically unrelated C major again sang in a manner that suggests we have changed into another key, raising the stakes again, but instead we return safely to the chord and home key of G major. This ride of a rising melody, tantalising the DNA with the possibility of uncertainty, but reaffirming its balance in several different mathematical configurations of chords and implied key changes, is a confident assertion that all is well. It states our mathematical configuration has been able to resolve itself three times, within three different circumstances in this short musical introduction. Three surges of pleasure will be experienced by the listener when he hears this for the first few times, which together with the words 'she loves you' leaves a feeling of warmth and optimism.

This song also illustrates another feature of music which is sometimes misused as an instrument of war. A single voice allows a song to remain personal and intimate. The addition of several voices in unison signifies strength and support as in the opening chorus line 'she loves you'. It adds to its power. DNA recognises these strengths and takes note. The addition of instruments has the same effect, especially with regard to the drum. The repetitive pounding of the atonal sound of the drum has no melody of optimism. The sound alone has many uncertainties attached to its atonal, rather flat musical quality. The steady rhythm causes the heart to beat in unison, to follow and match its pace, increasing your alertness as the blood is made to circulate faster, increasing our DNA's uncertainty. An amount of adrenaline may be released as a consequence. In this condition, it is easy to persuade us that something is wrong. Strong words of concern in the lyrics can be used to arouse our uncertainty into fear. It is only a short step to coerce the predisposed listener into actions of defence against the perceived threat. Follow this with the sound of a hundred voices singing in unison a song of war, and, of course, the rest will be history.

Games

A final example is to illustrate the control and effectiveness of the survival equation in games. Here, the problem is set out in the form of a new set of survival rules where we temporarily abandon the normal ones. The resolution is your physical or intellectual skill. The solution is to win. This simulates a high survival value since you have beaten the competition and secured your survival and your DNA's position above the competition. A wave of pleasure is guaranteed (Figure 44). Games are of many different types and thus can also work on other levels as well as the basic pleasure of winning. Football, like many other games, offers spatial-awareness puzzles, physical combat, the prize of a kill, that is, a goal (the goal simulating the kill in the hunt for food includes elation and aggression; notice in the photograph the raised fists).

THE ELATION OF WINNING

Figure 44

Chess offers mostly the same in terms of survival equations, with the obvious exception that the physical combat is more confined to imagery than real action. A crossword puzzle is a game of repeated small victories. As you process each clue, the resolution yields pleasure, with the added pleasure of a victory over the clue maker (the pleasure of beating the competition and solving the problem).

Such abstract simulations of survival equations are not allowed for long since long-term memory monitors how long this is going on and will eventually intrude into the process with a reminder that long experience suggests this is not 'real survival' and prods us into stopping. How many times has someone spent hours doing crosswords only to experience that feeling of 'wasted time' afterwards?

11

THE TRIPARTITE SYSTEM

The survival equation feeding the tripartite system is the basis for all our activities
There is an inbuilt policeman controlling our behaviour and happiness
It rewards us with pleasure for innovative ideas
Science, music, art, storytelling and so on

I could now consider the hypothesis that every idea and thought process we construct within our frontal lobe area of the brain was a survival equation, that is, we take in our observations and formulate within the 10-second concentration period a survival scenario or score. As described earlier, within the early infant's brain, the detail of a circle would be compressed or 'chunked' to save repetition; it seems likely that the survival scenario could also be 'chunked' or compressed as described in the previous chapter into a form of a ZIP file. By having a very short concentration period, it ensured new assessments were being made every 10 seconds. This would mean that every human being assembles a survival equation every 10 seconds of its waking and, to some extent sleeping, life. Like a rabbit when it feeds, our eyes and ears would be constantly checking that it's still safe out there. So that meant that the frontal lobe would be constantly performing survival equations.

But how was this connected to happiness? And how was this similarly connected to the old reptilian brain?

At this stage, I postulated the survival score might be considered in the same way to be a part of the 'fight-or-flight' process. In other words, the score not only included a danger level but also a positive message. It just needed to know the conclusion, which is the survival score. It didn't need to know the details. If the particular thought had a survival equation which generated a high survival value, then when it reached the old reptilian brain, it would send out a signal to release not only an appropriate amount of adrenaline but also the appropriate amount of dopamine from which we would derive both excitement and pleasure. This way we would feel happy when observing situations that have a potentially high survival value.

Thus, there must be some sort of survival equation to assess and judge the ever-changing risks to survival. There was no way that the brain had evolved for any other reason other than to ensure the survival of DNA. It wasn't an entertainment centre and it wasn't there just to admire the view. It was there to monitor the outside world for survival advantages and survival threats. So, having established this premise as a possibility, how did DNA evolve a survival equation to ensure its survival?

It is my hypothesis that at an early stage, during the development of the frontal lobe area, a similar development was made within the old reptilian brain together with the amygdala to link the production of dopamine from the 'flight-or-fight' mechanism. The link could also have stimulated substances producing anxiety as well as others producing pleasure, but for the ease of discussion, I will refer only to dopamine. This arrangement linking the frontal lobe with the old reptilian brain ('fight-or-flight') I have informally named 'the tripartite system'. It is essentially based on, and an extension of, the pain pleasure syndrome. (Figure 36) This association, I believed, controlled our happiness and our ultimate feeling of contentment.

Briefly, during the concentration time within the prefrontal lobe of a potentially high survival thought, it could signal via the old reptilian and amygdala complex the release of dopamine, producing a feeling of pleasure. Should this particular high-survival thought continue in our 10-second concentration period, we would experience repeated waves of happiness and optimism. After this concentration period is refreshed, another high survival thought may not necessarily follow, so more normal dopamine levels are re-established (dependent on the survival score of this next thought). Since the dopamine is a natural opiate, it acts like a drug and has a similar effect to another more dangerous opiate, heroin, so that when the dopamine level is restricted, so is our feeling of pleasure, and just like with any opiate drug, we feel uncomfortable.

This tripartite system also has another unique survival advantage in that pleasure could only be sustained for a few moments, perhaps 10 seconds, during the particular high survival thought. Repeating that exact thought would not generate any new pleasure since the idea had already been established and probably now sat in your long-term memory. One would have to modify this thought in some way to illustrate some additional benefit or invent a completely new survival idea before more opiate neurotransmitters such as dopamine or serotonin would be released. This 10-second limit had the important survival characteristic of maintaining our alertness.

The point was that under normal conditions, such neurotransmitters may only be supplied for a brief moment when realistic high survival scores existed in your concentration, that is, during the moment when we realised the high survival value of the thought. Even the final resulting achievement of the thought may not yield the same high level as the original idea. A typical illustration of how this could work would be as follows: We receive pleasure for the idea that the work we are doing towards an examination may give us unbounded additional security. Encouraged by this pleasure, we continue. However, after the moment we finally pass the exams and receive the certificate that we have qualified for, the level of pleasure is not that high anymore. The later celebration of the exam ceremony can be quite an anti-climax since the survival value was realised some time ago and is now fully established and has nothing new to offer.

Most celebrations take place well after the event, and as such, for the persons being honoured, it could be a confusing experience. The absence of direct dopamine injection at this stage could leave you feeling deflated during the celebration and at odds with the mood of the proceedings. Many who were trapped in these situations probably longed for the celebration to finish so that they could get on with something more challenging and consequently more pleasurable.

In other words, we receive pleasure for the 'process' of establishing a new idea with high survival value but not necessarily for the result. It also casts doubt on the wisdom of the expression that suggests we can relax and enjoy the fruits of our labours. In reality, we would never be allowed to relax since we are always on security duty. We could only truly enjoy the fruits of our 'processes'. This makes us work hard for our few moments of pleasure and ensures that everything we do is directed towards survival.

Any description or model concerning brain function would have to consider its primary purpose: that the brain is to secure DNA and its continuation into the future. Since DNA wishes to secure its survival above all others, it evolved the cerebral cortex to provide itself with a clearer picture of the outside world. All my deliberations, so far, point to this. However, despite this innovation, it appears that DNA doesn't want to lose the trusted old but reliable and proven system within the reptilian brain. It prefers to keep the final decision where it trusts the results, down in the reptilian brain complex. Employing a 'tripartite system', that is, the compression system of scores which summarises the survival scenarios from the evolving frontal lobe area, the 'fight-or-flight' mechanism of the brain stem controlling our adrenaline and dopamine reward procedure would have enabled DNA to keep a tight control on all our activities. It could ensure survival was the primary controlling mediator of all our thoughts and subsequent actions. So much so that perhaps all our thoughts and actions were in some way controlled by the tripartite system. To test this hypothesis, I began to examine our everyday thought processes and activities and to search for situations that might illustrate this relationship.

Let's take an example. A man with a passion for betting sees a race with one horse, and its odds are 100:1 to win. It's the only horse running, so it is bound to win. The frontal lobe processes this information and comes up with survival score of '10'. If he puts all his savings on this horse, he will increase his security 100 times. This message is sent down to the old reptilian brain where the DNA says, metaphorically, 'Yes, yes, this is a great idea', and to encourage him to go ahead, the reptilian brain sends a message not only for the hormone adrenaline but also for a high dose of the pleasure drug dopamine. The man, encouraged by this warm glow he experiences, rushes down to the race course to place a bet with all his hard-earned savings on this horse. Unfortunately, the horse falls at the first fence. Dutifully, the frontal lobe processes this new information into the 'survival equation' and comes up with a 'minus 10'. The message goes down to the reptilian brain complex, which decides to restrict all dopamine for the next year as punishment to discourage this kind of activity from ever happening again. In this case, DNA feels threatened by the loss of so much financial security indicated by the -10 score. So long as it didn't receive any other encouraging information, that is, a more positive and high-scoring survival equation, it would continue to feel fundamentally insecure and refuse to raise dopamine levels.

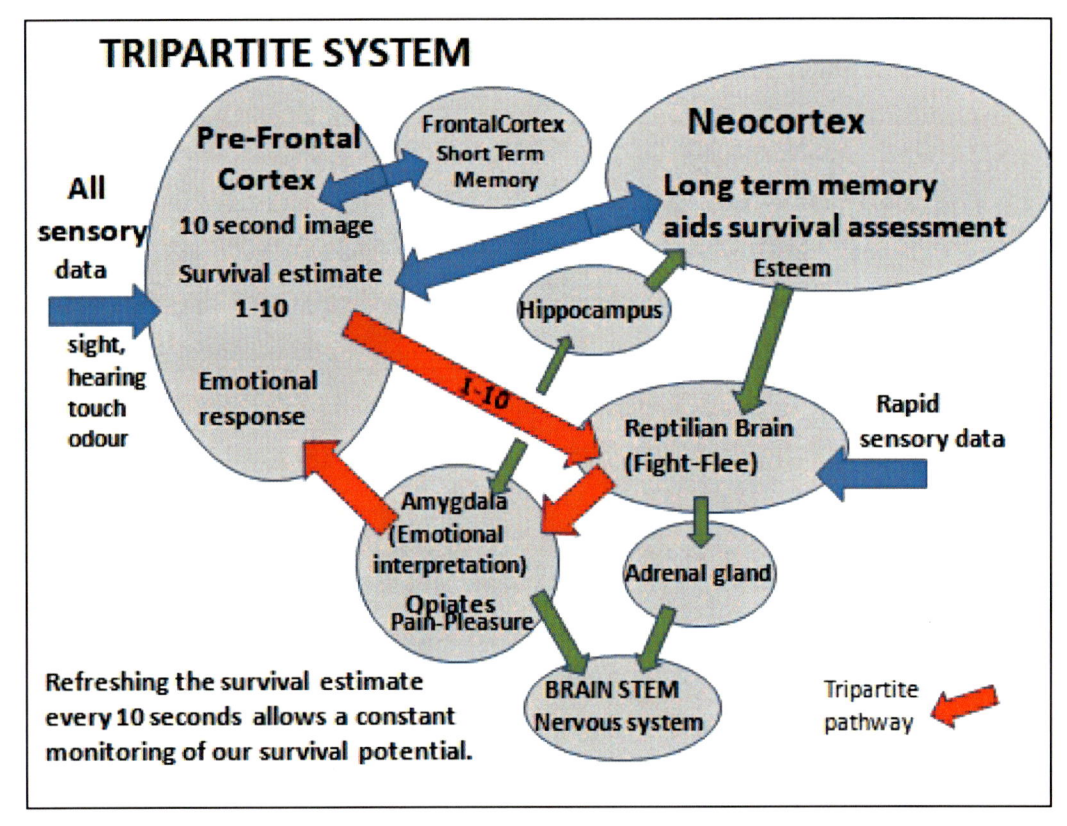

![Figure 45: Tripartite System diagram showing connections between Pre-Frontal Cortex (with "All sensory data" input from sight, hearing, touch, odour; 10 second image, Survival estimate 1-10, Emotional response), Frontal Cortex Short Term Memory, Neocortex (Long term memory aids survival assessment, Esteem), Hippocampus, Amygdala (Emotional interpretation), Reptilian Brain (Fight-Flee) with Rapid sensory data input, Opiates Pain-Pleasure, Adrenal gland, and Brain Stem Nervous system. Note: "Refreshing the survival estimate every 10 seconds allows a constant monitoring of our survival potential." Red arrows indicate Tripartite pathway.]

Figure 45

The model I am now able to present provides a basic 'tripartite' mechanism able to steer our body through the trials and tribulations of its everyday existence to ensure survival. The direct link from the frontal lobe area where the survival equations are constructed, to the old reptilian brain complex where the survival values are translated into various forms of motivators, provided an inbuilt system designed to encourage or discourage our survival strategy. Dopamine, the happiness drug (with perhaps others), would be released as a part of the neurotransmitters produced in the reptilian brain and amygdala to encourage us to proceed with enthusiasm or it would be restricted with the opposite consequences.

Hormones such as adrenaline could be added as needed to meet the necessary speed of action and other special body requirements. This link is schematically represented in Figure 45 and represents beautifully balanced picture of a survival machine.

In addition to the highs and lows of our pain and pleasure, there is a neutral position when the opiates are not actively changing our mood. A period I would refer to as 'contentment'. This 'middle position' may exist for extended periods of time determined by the previous sequence of dopamine activity. A repeated series of dopamine highs would tend to favour a feeling of mild pleasure; in other words, contentment. A repeated series of dopamine withdrawal would leave us feeling discontented. Obviously, we would prefer contentment which possibly represents the ultimate goal for all humanity..... 'Survival of the Contented'. (Figure 46)

None of the above needs us to be the fittest as suggested by Darwin's 'Survival of the Fittest'. Unfortunately, the word 'fittest' implies physical strength without regard to its environment. Physical strength alone will not guarantee survival and contentment within a hostile environment. Survival and contentment are more likely achieved within a safe and supportive environment.

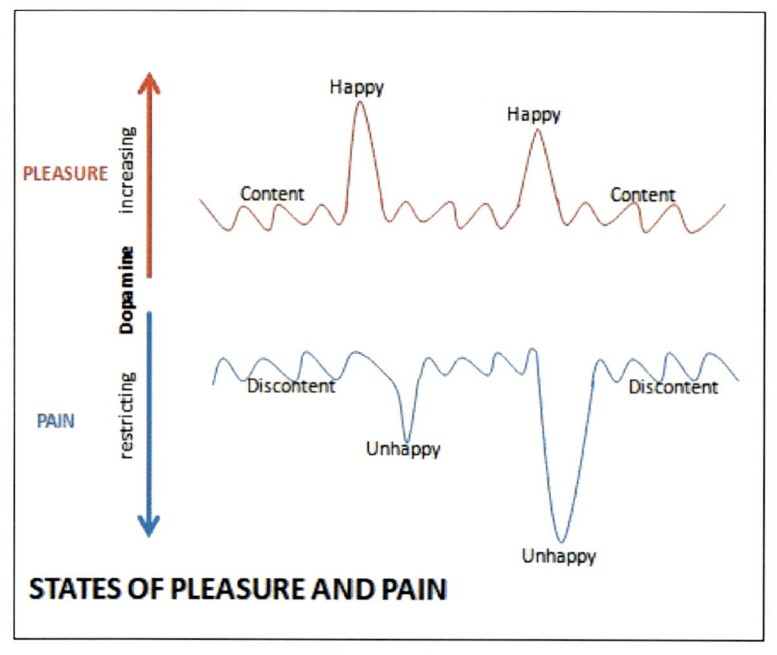

Figure 46

12

COOL DUDES AND WIMPS

Strength of signal may determine our personality

A COUPLE OF COOL DUDES

Figure 47

The potential of the tripartite system was not fully exhausted yet. As I began to toy with the various permutations this system offered, there appeared to be further consequences with regard to our personality. My mind was drawn to previous observations concerning so-called strong and weak personalities. I was always impressed by the ability of certain individuals to be gregarious and charismatic, to become leaders and to be the centre of attention wherever they went. Others, by contrast, would spend their whole life in the shadows as rather nervous individuals, reclusive, shying away from larger groups of people, preferring just their own company or singular friends. At this time, the expression 'cool dudes' was often used to describe those with these charismatic qualities, and 'wimps' was used for those who were more nervous and reclusive. It seemed everyone wanted to be a cool dude. Nobody would really choose to be a wimp. Giles, with his impressive control of oratory, was our college guru-like character and fit the typical 'cool dude'. He was not only charismatic; he was also clever, wily and shrewd. However, a brief perusal of a few more examples could show a complete range of intellect associated within each group. Similarly, these groups did not necessarily equate with 'good guys' and 'bad guys'. For example, we would have to include the leaders of the manic religious cults and the local groups of football hooligans in the category of the 'cool dudes' as well as well-respected leaders such as a prime minister or president. In the same way, we could include the introverted character of a reluctantly famous scientist, composer, poet or author in the category of 'wimps' as well as those who merely prefer to hide away from society. So why these distinct groups of personalities? What really decides which type you would eventually be?

One other observation also intrigued me. It was best illustrated by a colleague of mine and his brother. Their difference in age was only one and a half years, hardly anything. Yet whenever they would sit down to watch a film, the younger brother would be guaranteed to be weeping at the slightest appearance of a sad or emotive scene. The elder brother would be completely unmoved and stare at his younger brother in amazement, wondering what all the fuss was about. He could watch any type of violence or emotive scene without an apparent care. Such differences between people are common and perhaps symptomatic of some underlying control of our behaviour.

With this in mind, it occurred to me that some of these characteristics might be naturally inherited from the 'tripartite system'. I remember this was a particularly exciting concept at the time, as it seemed to offer a potentially simple controlling mechanism in operation. What follows is not intended to be the definitive answer with regard to the controlling mechanisms of such personality characteristics; it merely opens up a possible area of influence not previously considered. So let's take a look at this concept and how I believed it might control this part of our basic personality.

Signal Strength

As with all biological mechanisms, some are more efficient than others. It is a machine like anything else, and in each one of us, it works a little bit better or worse than in others (Figure 48).

PERSONALITY TRAITS

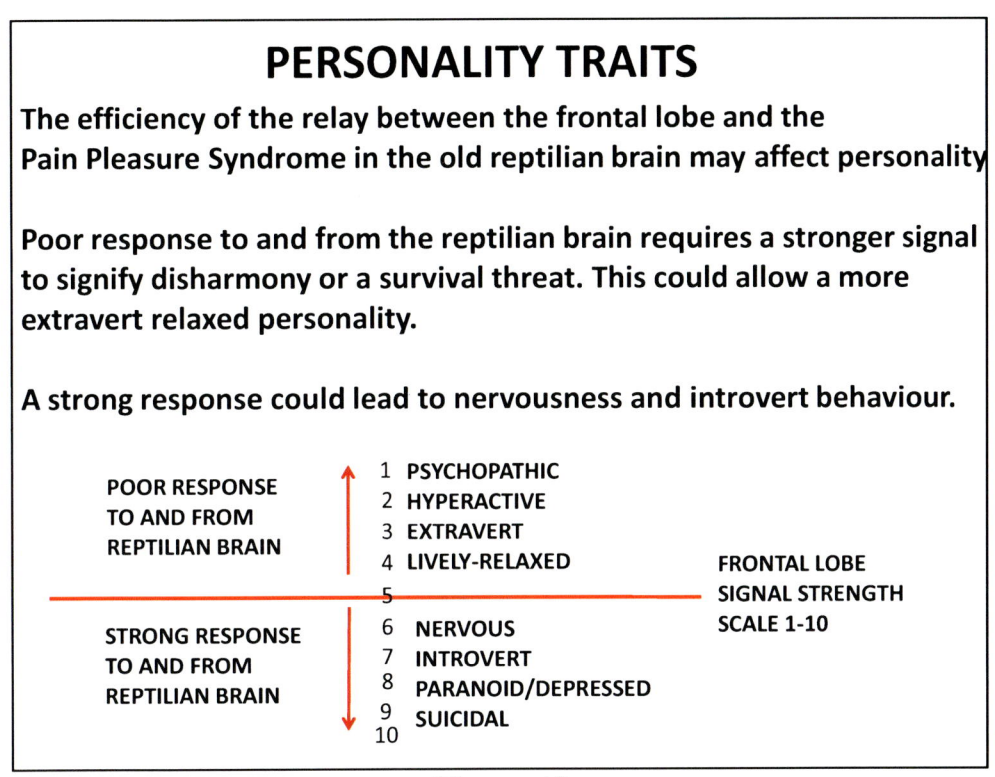

The efficiency of the relay between the frontal lobe and the Pain Pleasure Syndrome in the old reptilian brain may affect personality

Poor response to and from the reptilian brain requires a stronger signal to signify disharmony or a survival threat. This could allow a more extravert relaxed personality.

A strong response could lead to nervousness and introvert behaviour.

POOR RESPONSE TO AND FROM REPTILIAN BRAIN	1 PSYCHOPATHIC 2 HYPERACTIVE 3 EXTRAVERT 4 LIVELY-RELAXED 5	FRONTAL LOBE SIGNAL STRENGTH SCALE 1-10
STRONG RESPONSE TO AND FROM REPTILIAN BRAIN	6 NERVOUS 7 INTROVERT 8 PARANOID/DEPRESSED 9 SUICIDAL 10	

Figure 48

Let's consider what would happen if the connections between the frontal lobe processor and the reptilian brain did vary and were a little stronger than normal. Recently this variation in efficiency has been recognised as 'motor latency'. The strength of this signal I have schematically represented by a scale of 1–10 (please note this is not the same as the survival score 1–10). Employing this scale, this person would experience slightly more pleasure for a particular experience, but at the same time, he would receive more pain. This would tend to make the person a little excitable and also a little nervous because he would probably receive the pain as self-criticism. Such a person would be on the insecure side and perhaps a little pessimistic since for all the pleasure he receives, he experiences reasonable amounts of pain, which makes him apprehensive of the consequences of pleasure. Very often as a consequence such persons put an extensive series of buffers or defence mechanisms in the way of anything they do to protect themselves. Such people can make good scientists since they get very excited about their results but at the same time get very worried that the results are actually correct. Below is an attempt to identify these behavioural characteristics in known personalities.

Strong Signal

If we increase the strength of the signal further, then the person would tend to worry excessively. He would feel his emotions very strongly. The self-criticism initiated by low survival scores would lead them to hide their excitability, which they would regard as an embarrassing display of uncontrolled behaviour. Such people would withdraw into themselves and become introverted. They may often become creative, artists, musicians and so on, since their withdrawal is counteracted by a need to still express themselves and the strong emotions inside them. Based on film and literature (Lewisohn, 1986), an example of such a person could be Paul McCartney (Figure 49).

PAUL MACARTNEY WORRIED AND HESITANT

Figure 49

His smiling persona clearly displays moments when excitement is obviously bubbling up inside him. This might lead him on to feel very happy and content within himself. However, at these moments his statements could seem a little arrogant and self-congratulating, urged on by the strong signals of pleasure he might receive at that time

As he begins to hear his own words becoming excessive and less well considered, he often pauses, as uncertainty and doubt appear in his mind (Figure 49). The survival value of his conversation constantly being scrutinised by the frontal lobe is now being restricted, and signals of discomfort are now racing to the fore. His words appear to backtrack, attempting to counter the excessive emotion displayed seconds earlier. He will retreat from the scene feeling very uncomfortable trying desperately to control this rollercoaster ride. As a consequence, we see him as a person capable of great flamboyance but great privacy. His privacy he holds dearly, protecting this above all. He does this by never displaying his 'true feelings' within any sort of public arena. The words we hear from him are an act, a performance. They would not be his real opinions or feelings. The locking away of his true feelings is the introversion. He tells us what he thinks we want to hear. He feels more secure in displaying the strength of his true feelings within a song. In this context, he would have the time to consider and judge his statements and decide whether he is comfortable with it. This affords him more control.

Another feature that would likely be a result of these strong signals is that the person would be quick to get angry. If the person should be crossed or just frustrated by not being able to get his or her own way, the signal of anger would rise very quickly and strongly. Such people would have to apply a strong measure of self-control to subdue this emotion, and they often do. Otherwise they would rapidly appear threatening and abusive. This is another reason why such people become introverted. To save them the embarrassing apologies that will inevitably follow after an outburst of such behaviour. Similarly, after a certain amount of alcohol, it would be easy to lose a tight control. The natural survival bar is lowered by the alcohol, which can now allow embarrassing scenes of overconfidence. A short time after the effects of alcohol subside, and the survival bar returns to is normal level, the inevitable awareness of such behaviour can begin a whole series of self-inflicted criticisms, as the dopamine is restricted.

More severe signals may create more exaggerated feelings of concern and happiness as the levels of opiates are increased and decreased. The person feels incapable of coping with his emotions and can appear neurotic in his behaviour. He or she may apply odd procedures to try and counter-balance the extremes of pain and pleasure they can receive within a relatively short period and for what should be normal situations for others. These odd procedures can become obsessive, as they try to increase the procedure in an attempt to protect themselves from the extremes they feel. Such extremes can lead to instability and in some cases suicide since in a period of extreme excitability they can become suddenly very depressed. The opiate influx and restriction during all the above behavioural scenarios provide only a rollercoaster ride of pain and pleasure.

Weak Signal
From the above model I was convinced I was not only understanding the dynamics controlling happiness but also developing a basis for understanding 'traits' within our personality. So let's continue to explore other consequences of the model.

For example, if people were born with a lowered strength in the connection between the old reptilian brain and the frontal lobe, then a whole host of new personality traits could be explained. A slight decrease in strength would lower the level of pleasure but at the same time lower the level of discomfort from pain and self-criticism. Such people would tend to be more light-hearted and jovial, more free to speak and act outrageously, not having to fear the consequences of severe restriction of opiates and the consequent self-criticism.

An example of a person that fits these criteria could be John Lennon (Figure 50). Where Paul McCartney could be flamboyant and feel uncomfortable, John Lennon wouldn't care.

He could say, and did say in public, some of the most outrageous statements of that time, culminating in the infamous 'The Beatles are more popular than Christ'. He would deliberately throw himself into controversy and not flinch. He did this because he wanted to feel things. Because his signal was weaker, he didn't enjoy the private moments of being alone with his own thoughts. In such quiet situations, he felt very little in terms of excitement. Instead, he would go out into the world to deliberately provoke debate to feel something, to push his lower levels of opiates higher. It would be highly unlikely that John could sit quietly with a stamp album and enjoy the beauty and history that lay behind such objects. This would not provide enough opiate response.

A DIRECT COOL STARE WITHOUT FEAR OR HESITATION

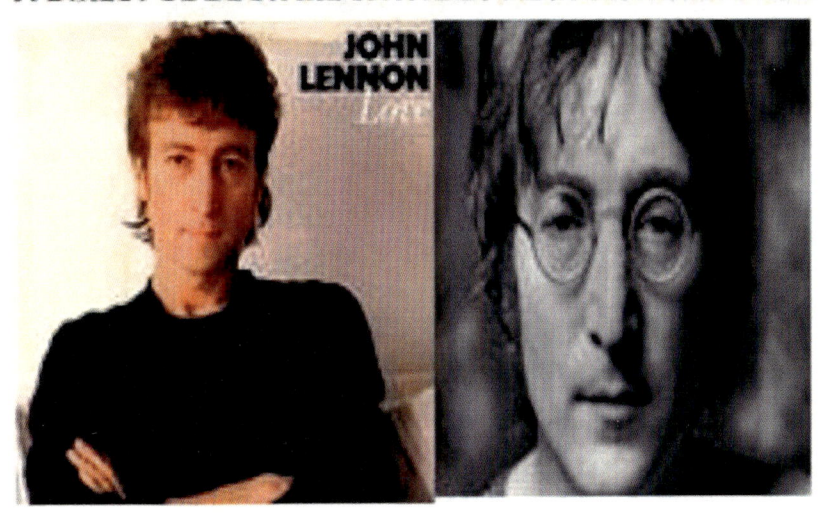

Figure 50

However, it is not impossible to envisage Paul taking a trip into the countryside to just to be alone with his own thoughts and privately enjoy the natural beauty of the plants and wildlife. John appears always to have been looking for confrontation, not because he really wanted to cause trouble but because only then could he actually feel something. Telling somebody the honest truth to their face takes guts. Why? Not because it is intellectually difficult to put the words together but because most of us fear the consequences of the opiate response. Those of us with stronger signals would not wish to cause the other person pain, and we would fear the consequent remorse in terms of self-criticism of our provocative action. In addition, we would fear the threat to ourselves in terms of physical and mental pain if the person fought back with equally hurtful statements about us or with physical blows to the body. John could forego all that for the pleasure of feeling the adrenaline and dopamine he received for setting himself above the person he had confronted. Just as in a game, the process of winning sets you above the competition and you earn the dopamine. The sight of this confronted person feeling uncomfortable in front of him might not particularly affect him since the signals indicating possible dangers of reprisal were weak. The withdrawal of dopamine would not be as great as those with stronger signals. John could say and do what he liked in full view of the media to get the rush of winning. As a result, he became a great self-publicist. The public loved this because this was the real John Lennon he was exposing, raw and naked, not an act like Paul's simulated flamboyancy. They admired him because of this. They could see he was laying himself open and totally vulnerable. People admire bravery, and John got an extra rush of dopamine for the support and security the admiration gave his DNA. As a consequence, he played the part to the full and became the legend we know. To some degree, he will have experienced pain but nothing he couldn't handle. Consequently, when he did complain of any suffering, he was able to enjoy the sympathy of his admirers who, comparing it to their own standards, imagined far worse than was really going on in his mind. The more forceful nature of his music and lyrics also may reflect the weaker signal. They had to be exciting for him to feel the benefit. Incidentally many hard-rock musicians have characteristics that fit the weaker signal, which may thus correspond with their need to play extremely exciting raw, basic music. Even his ballads had raw and strong emotional lyrics. Nothing was kept back. He was not afraid.

A further decrease would allow the people to be even more extravert. At the same time, such people would be less excitable, more cool and collected. They could take even more criticism. This would allow them the luxury of being able to focus on the purely intellectual side of the matter at hand rather than be inhibited by the constant surges and withdrawals of dopamine. In times of emotional crises, such people would be able to think clearly, remain calm and make unpopular decisions without any great discomfort to themselves. For example, such people could become leaders and politicians. Two leaders who appeared to display these characteristics were Sir Winston Churchill and Dame Margaret Thatcher.

Churchill was a gifted orator and intellectual. He was also reported to be an extravert who enjoyed being the centre of attention and being in the limelight. This combination caused him to be very popular on the dinner circuit since he was famous for his brutal outspokenness and unpredictability. For all the reasons John Lennon did what he did, so did Churchill. Churchill also was able to display another attribute associated with the weaker signal. He was able to make decisions involving the life and death of thousands of soldiers (and civilians) on the basis of cold logic, unaffected by the distractions of uncontrollable fear and remorse. The bigger the decision, the more adrenaline and dopamine he could feel. In less extraverted persons, such decisions would be engulfed with great waves of adrenaline and dopamine followed by massive withdrawals to the extent they would be overcome with excitement one minute and grim fear the next. Within Churchill, they were probably weaker, and as a consequence, the extremes were manageable and even pleasurable, whilst leaving him still with a cool head to steer us through the crises of wartime. Such combinations of the weaker signal together with intellect are the hallmarks of great leaders. This does not mean that occasionally the totality of it all would not get through to him. I am suggesting a weaker signal, not the absence of such. Churchill was known to have suffered from 'the black dog', a phrase he used to describe his periods of depression. There must have been reflective moments, as with John Lennon, perhaps appearing as low values of esteem, when he was left without the dopamine generated from the admiring crowds and the rushes of decision-making. Here, alone with reality, and without these supports, there was only restriction of the supporting opiates. However, he managed these serious challenges when others would not have been able to. One of his close colleagues and confidants during these warring years was not able to cope and succumbed to suicide.

Margaret Thatcher, according to recent literature (Campbell, 2009) was not such a gifted orator or intellectual. Her personality lacked wit and humour, and she was not an overly popular figure amongst the public during her time in office as prime minister. The media would ridicule her bossy and school-mistress mannerisms. She still possessed, however, the same salient characteristics that make a good leader. A weaker signal would allow her to ignore the criticisms and enabled her to focus ruthlessly on the application of her thoughts and ideas. Like all politicians, she was able to sacrifice her own personal pride to climb the greasy political pole all the way to the top. Most of us cannot do this. There are too many withdrawals of dopamine as we begin to suffer character attacks and assassinations from colleagues. Maggie was able to resist all these attempts to break down her will. She was also able, just like Lennon and Churchill, to stand up squarely to confrontation and speak her mind. These attributes, together with a clever appreciation of the political games around her, enabled her to survive and gain admirers and support. Less able politicians, weakened by their stronger signals, could stand behind her and be shielded from the extremes of political pressure. This way, she gained further support for her cause. As she grew more powerful she also showed an ability to make hard and ruthless decisions, just like Churchill, involving the careers and lives of thousands of others. Such characteristics, I believe, clearly suggest personality traits governed by the weaker signal.

The suggestion that less able politicians, weakened by their stronger signals, could stand behind her is a principle I informally refer to as the 'umbrella syndrome', which can be observed in other areas of life.

An example that involves the umbrella syndrome can be seen active in the formation of 'teenage gangs'. The natural leaders in these gangs most likely possess the weaker signal and are perfect for the sort of confrontation teenagers indulge in as they challenge the establishment. The rest of the gang members would usually possess varying levels of stronger signals and would shelter behind the leader only daring sporadically to risk the emotional and physical consequences of outspoken confrontation.

Besides these examples of personality traits and behavioural characteristics discussed, there are further hypothetical stages to be reached along this trend of a weakening signal. For example, as the connection weakens further, the person would receive little pleasure from normal activities and would probably have to carry out an extreme action to get a 'buzz' of emotion. At the same time, because of lowered pain levels, a person would be free to carry out these extreme actions without fear of too much pain from self-criticism. These people would most likely appear extremely brave, being able to climb precarious mountains, carry out dangerous tasks and more or less feel free to say or do exactly what they feel. People who could fall into this category could include, for example, the builders of tall skyscrapers, mountaineers, certain types of soldiers and firemen. They perform tasks that require an ice-cool calm head. You cannot afford to get overexcited or disturbed by the extreme rushes or withdrawals of dopamine and adrenaline. It seems likely to me that such people with weak signals are actually able to enjoy the job because they experience at least some pleasure, as the extreme circumstances they are in eventually provide enough signal.

It is probably the same for base jumping, sky diving and other extremely dangerous sports. I have heard it suggested that doing this type of sport automatically provides you with the reward of high amounts of dopamine. This, I believe, is a dangerous and incorrect understanding of the situation. The implication of this interpretation suggests that there is a simple relationship between the amount of reward you receive and the amount of danger you subject yourself to. It also suggests that the bigger the risk, the longer the reward will be sustained afterwards. In my opinion, this is not the case. The person who initiated the sport of freefall leaping off high rock precipices is probably one with a very weak signal. His head was free from fear, and when he falls, his mind is clear to steer himself down and pull the ripcord at the appropriate moment. The process of properly steering himself as he falls, the proper management of his equipment, his realisation that he has pulled the ripcord at the correct moment to open the parachute and has saved his life and the life of his DNA will be rewarded with high dopamine and adrenaline. He will experience some fear as he falls and some joy as he opens the parachute. After that moment, the rush is over and he has to do it again to feel what is for him a rare moment of joy. It is only during the process of realisation that the dopamine will rise. Shortly afterwards he will return to normal. At all times these levels he can manage because no matter how extreme the circumstance, his signal is considerably weaker than that of the average person.

If a person who experiences stronger signals, even in everyday situations, is encouraged to attempt such a jump with the idea he will get a reward of high ecstasy, he may instead get a shock. Even if he manages to get to the edge, the sense of fear will be almost unbearable (Figure 51).

DNA will be doing its utmost to stop you from going over the edge. The messages it receives all add up to suicide, and it will try to immobilise you such that you will not be able to move. It will withdraw all your dopamine and set up a whole load of adrenaline ready and waiting if needed. This combination of frozen automotive functions, poised with adrenaline and the lack of dopamine, would leave you feeling extremely uncomfortable. If you did manage to go over the edge, you would most likely not be able to coordinate yourself, lose control and fail to pull the ripcord. Should you manage to reach the ground safely, you would probably experience shock. After your DNA has experienced such extreme and strong life-threatening messages, it demands to be reassured that all is well.

THE JUMP

Figure 51

This phenomena of shock is similar to and yet the opposite of the 'joke' process. A normal message of security has been followed by apparently illogical messages of extreme stress and danger. During this period, it checks and rechecks, each time receiving further life-threatening messages to its survival. When the signal is strong, the stress responses would be equally as strong. It would be the same for all types of life-threatening attacks or experiences and is to be entirely expected. DNA is like the crew of a submarine. It cannot really see, hear or feel. It relies on us, the host, that is, our cell contents, to act as the periscope and provide it with information. When apparently normal life circumstances are devastatingly changed without warning, DNA responses within the nucleus become totally disoriented. It doesn't really know what went wrong and how it managed to allow the host to get it into such a life-threatening situation. It has no alternative course of action other than to withdraw the dopamine and shut down all activities other than those that are absolutely essential until completely reassured it is back in control, as would any computer receiving contradictory signals.

A further hypothesis concerning the weaker signal could explain the aggressive behaviour of some hyperactive children. In such cases, they would have a lot of ideas and energy but little self-criticism to control them. They might break their toys and physically hurt their friends or pets since it would take such extreme actions to stir any emotions within them. Without the feeling of remorse, they have no tool to indicate this behaviour is inappropriate. Similarly, normal behaviour provides little or no pleasure. They have nothing to steer them towards appropriate behaviour.

Consider a further extreme when there is no signal. These people could be called 'flat liners'. They could be totally amoral and able to carry out extreme acts of cruelty without receiving any signal of pain from the brain. No matter what the score of the survival equation, they would not receive any pleasure or pain as a consequence. It would be a barren and cold world for them observing the strange emotional behaviour and reactions of others only with a sense of curiosity and intellectual interest. Even eating and drinking would hold no pleasure, such functions being motivated automatically by the old reptilian brain by its more direct route excluding the frontal lobe. Without the emotional control, they would ruthlessly pursue their self-interests without compassion or empathy for those around them until someone stopped them. They would be predisposed towards crime should the circumstances arise. They could be intelligent and thus extremely manipulative. Indeed, such 'flat liners' could be envisaged as dangerous and are expected to develop psychopathic tendencies. Dictators such as Milosevic and Stalin appear to fit these characteristics. The few close-up images shown on television reveal facial signals supporting a cold unemotional detachment from the proceedings going on around them. The few descriptions of their personalities suggest they are men of few words, always scheming and able to give out instructions of mass murder without compunction. It means nothing to them emotionally that they are responsible for the deliberate murder of thousands of men, women and children. They only look at the number and then, with equal coldness of logic, consider if the numbers of the dead were high enough.

Another example that came to light, after the writing of this manuscript, which may fit this hypothesis is the terrible case of Dr Shipman, a general practitioner from the UK who managed to deliberately kill over 200 of his patients without any apparent reason. Could it be that his only motive was to obtain the weakest signal of pleasure that he could receive from achieving these murders without detection? In his cold emotional world, it would have been just a game. His arrest and the subsequent court proceedings and newspaper reports all deploring his evil conduct would, for him, be just an inconvenience, preventing him to continue with the one thing that gave him a little bit of pleasure.

Clearly this sliding scale of signal between the reptilian brain and the frontal lobe could predispose people to the varying types of personality we often encounter. The difference between the basic types could be, perhaps, illustrated by envisaging two persons, representing the strong and weaker signal, viewing a highly emotive TV program. As described earlier, the person with strong signals tends to end up with a handkerchief whilst the one with weaker signals might sit there finishing his bag of crisps wondering what all the fuss is about. It is well-known that some people, both men and women, will appear to cry at almost anything, a feature I would attribute to a stronger signal. It would appear that a prerequisite of being a 'cool dude' in this world is to have weaker connections and a 'wimp' to have stronger signals.

Such personality traits also extend themselves to the animal kingdom. My family had two black cats of the same age from identical backgrounds. One was the cool dude, called George; the other was a paranoid nervous wreck called Arthur. They both lived together for many years. George was very sociable, afraid of nothing, liked to fight and stayed out all day before coming home and stretching out full length in front of the fire. Arthur was extremely cautious, very unsociable, spent most of his time hidden behind the sofa or high up on top of a cupboard and rarely liked to go out. George liked to tease Arthur. When George left by the cat flap in the door, he waited just outside the door for Arthur to follow, and when he did, George pounced, giving Arthur a nasty fright. George didn't really hurt Arthur; he just liked to tease.

The difference between these two cats' personalities seems to fit the effects of the strong and weak signal. Arthur had the strong signal and was consequently nervous and preferred to be alone in a safe place. George, however, had a weaker signal, was less fearful, more playful and sociable. A good example of his lack of fear was illustrated during one of our moves. As he went about setting out his new territory, he set up one of his 'signing posts' in the middle of a (not-too-busy) crossroads. He would sit there awhile, licking himself and watching with interest the cars as they whizzed either side of him, without any sign of alarm.

13

OTHER FACTORS

Personality traits
Anger, empathy
Subconscious
Esteem-Conscience: Our Inner Policeman

Despite the clear evidence to suggest that the strong and weak signals affect our personality, it seemed other factors such as hormones and the environment (stability, affluence) may exaggerate or subdue these characteristics. Some early childhood experiences may predispose us to respond to a circumstance in a particular manner independent of signal strength. Nevertheless, despite these possible influences, it is my experience from observing the personalities I have encountered that the efficiency of these connections, together with the level of intelligence, is the prime relationship that forms our personality.

I also attempted a very dangerous exercise of describing the sensitive area of personality types and how the tripartite system and signal strength might be influential. I realise this can be a very contentious area, but the personality types described are intended only as a mechanism to illustrate the concept.

A diagram illustrating signal strength against the likely level of intelligence is shown in Figure 52. High intelligence is described as a high perception ability whereas low intelligence is equated with low perception abilities. The diagram then places the likely location of the personality traits that could be equated to a particular ratio of these two variables. The centre line showing the varying strength of signal 1–10, displays the personality traits discussed above. To the left of this line are the traits that are envisaged to appear if the person is thought to be above-average intelligence. So let's begin again to consider the possible effects.

As discussed, some scientists, artists and writers would appear to fit the stronger signal. Artists are spontaneous and create their own original material. The lower half of this diagram may well be dominated by creative personalities all introverted but still eager to express themselves.

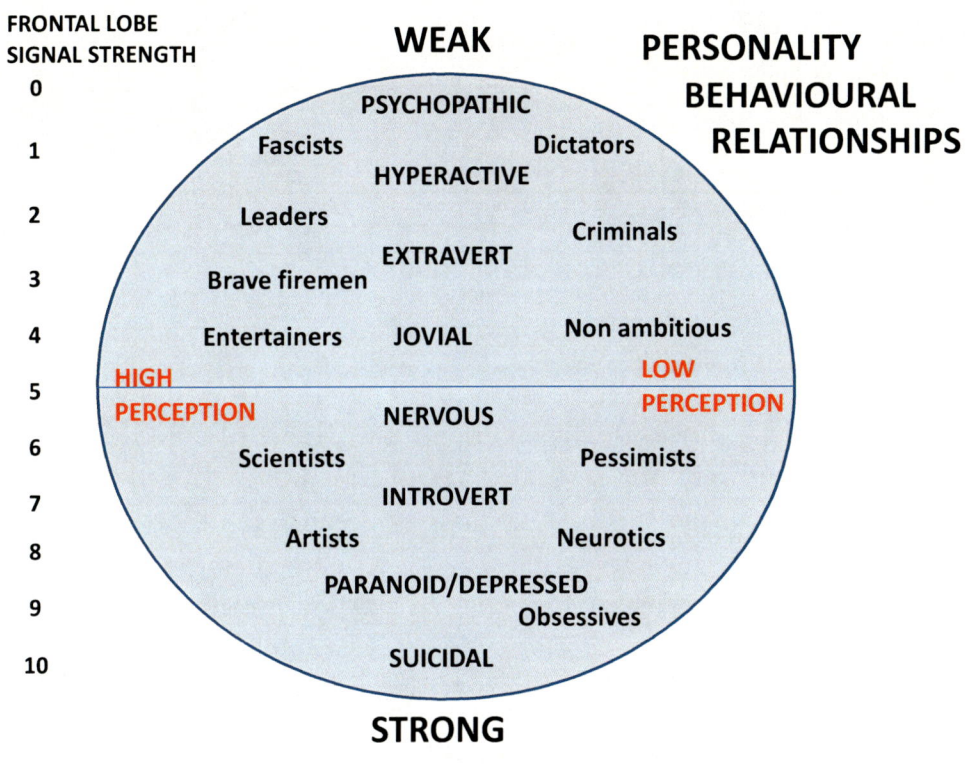

Figure 52

As the signal begins to weaken, the more light-hearted in nature would lend itself to entertainers and actors. These are craftsmen rather than artists. They tend to use prearranged material made by others. Entertainers and actors need a reasonably good ability to observe human behaviour and a cool head to be able to deliver rehearsed lines and perform the behavioural characteristics convincingly. Some of the more contemporary artists also fit into this category but not as a rule.

In this area of the weaker signal, the academic world might generate engineers instead of creative scientists. These people build and skilfully apply the rules rather than design them. Further along this weakening trend could appear accountants, surgeons, auditors, leaders, lawyers and finally, dictators.

If we now could consider what happens along this trend when the individual has a lower level of perception, the following personality traits might appear: A slightly stronger signal to those less able to understand the pattern of their emotions might result in a gloomy, pessimistic persona. The slightly higher return of pain for every occasion of pleasure would cause them to moan and complain fairly regularly such that it becomes irritating to others around them. As the signal increases, the less perceptive would perhaps be at a loss of how to deal with the problems and could, as discussed before, appear neurotic, with the inevitable protective buffer mechanisms. There are a variable number of such buffers which could become more frequent and obsessive in persons with stronger signals and lower perception abilities.

On the other side of this line, as the signal begins to weaken, the less perceptive person as well as being more light-hearted could become less ambitious. It is a commonly observed combination to see individuals who are out of work, and not seeking work, who are apparently jovial and content. Conversations show an ability to perceive some of the problems they face, but there appears to be no will to change these circumstances even when help is offered. The balance of signal appears to allow a certain resignation to their circumstance. The pain signal indicating lack of security to and from the DNA via the tripartite system might be just too weak to disturb their few comforts.

As the signal weakened, I envisaged that the lack of emotional stimulus together with a lack of intellect would leave the individual without humour and ambition and as a consequence appear introverted. The introvert with a 'strong signal' would be the result of suppressed emotions and, as a consequence, if primed or fed with alcohol, could become suddenly very animated and talkative to the extent of becoming boring. By contrast, introverts generated from a weaker signal might show cold indifference if spoken to and remain introverted at all times. If primed with alcohol, they would most likely tend to become even more morose.

Further along the 'weak trend' appear the extremely brave, which appear to be of a variety of intellectual abilities. It could be hypothesised that there are some differences, but essentially their lack of fear coupled with the pleasure they gain could allow them to do the most daring of tasks.

When I talked to a very brave fireman and his wife, he began to tell of how he had just decided to leave work and threatened not to return in protest against some new procedures being introduced at the fire station. His wife was horrified and clearly concerned. He, on the other hand, was totally 'cool' and undisturbed and was willing to take the risk – a clear example, perhaps, of this weaker signal in action.

Unfortunately, within this weaker signal area, such people may also be predisposed to criminal behaviour. If personal circumstances within their life, be it lack of money, improper peer pressure or bad judgement, steer them in this direction, they are readily capable of performing criminal and even violent acts. The lower the intellect, the more this is likely.

The above patterns represent the theoretical consequences of a varying signal strength emanating from the frontal lobe and the reptilian brain complex areas. It shows how this 'variable', together with intellectual ability, could significantly affect our personality. But do I really believe it? Could there be alternative and more credible explanations for the personality traits just described? Are these differences better explained by the more traditional concepts of childhood experience, parental influence and peer pressure?

For example, an oppressed childhood with dominating parental control is likely to yield a person with an introverted nature, afraid to cross boundaries set by authority. To some extent, I have to agree that this influence has an effect. However, such influence would be marked conspicuously upon a child with stronger signals but not necessarily on a child with weaker ones. This difference has been noted in recent psychological studies (Bergen University) of children who come from disturbed backgrounds (Den Levetann barn – 'the dandelion children'). Despite their difficult background, some of the children go on to be well balanced and successful individuals within society whilst others clearly do not. In this case, could it be the difference within their signal strength that caused these personality traits rather than the impact of their background?

A similar detachment from the surrounding environment is suggested in cases where children are adopted into a family where the parents sometimes show problematic personality characteristics. In such circumstances, I have been able to observe, first-hand, that the children develop totally untouched by these characteristics and appear to have emerged with quite distinct and well-balanced personalities of their own.

The most striking evidence that the major traits of our personalities are predetermined rather than learned has been presented in studies of identical twins. These studies showed that despite being separated at birth and placed in totally different families and home environments, they displayed very few differences in personality traits at a later age. It can even be shown that such twins took up similar careers, pastimes and lifestyles. These observations suggested very little influence from the surrounding environment and tend to support the hypothesis proposed earlier in this chapter. That is not to negate the importance of proper parenting, which is essential to create a good character and socially capable human on top of these underlying personality traits.

One final comment: I have always admired those who appear to be cool and calm in all situations and have the intellect to act wisely despite the circumstances. If it is merely a learning process, surely it is possible, as an intelligent adult, to relearn some of the basic attributes required to be 'cool'. Yet despite knowing the parameters, I have still never been able to emulate them. The strength of fear or concern overrides any intellectual ability to remain calm. This can be illustrated in another way. As children, we could be frightened of riding on the more extreme rides in a fairground whilst others could endure such experiences and even enjoy them. In adult life, we should be able to modulate our fear and approach these rides more rationally. However, for most people, it remains the same stressful experience, and they are not able to control this fear whilst others can continue to enjoy the situation as before.

The most persuasive evidence that earlier experience controls our later behaviour comes from differences in sibling personalities. Very often the first-born in the family assumes authority and leadership qualities whereas the youngest is more free-spirited and laidback from carrying less responsibility. These qualities at first sight appear to contradict the previous thesis above. However, the qualities just described may still not correlate with coolness or nervousness. Eldest brothers and sisters can be quite paranoid and nervous about their roles. Equally younger siblings can aspire to become leaders. As discussed earlier, concerning the 'dandelion children', signal strength will emphasise or exacerbate any externally learned traits in their personality.

In the personality traits I was able to describe, there appears very little room for charity, for the unselfish, dedicated life to a humanitarian and worthy cause. Where is the compassion expressed in this philosophy? There were many who devoted and sacrificed a great part of their lives for others, apparently without complaint. It is very difficult to be critical in such areas without feeling some sense of guilt and that somehow we are treading upon sacred ground. However, in our desire to be reverent about such situations, we tend to ignore any other features that may infringe upon this reverence. Sometimes, in our eagerness to preserve our image, we will raise the status to an exalted level, a level possibly not entirely consistent with the reality. Mother Theresa, for example, dedicated her life entirely to the care and welfare of others. How could anyone suggest she was anything but compassionate and unselfish? We conjure up an image of a kindly woman, always gentle, always caring. But was this actually true? And does it really matter? She got the job done and that's what counts.

As I have described before, we can care for very selfish reasons. I am not suggesting there is any malice behind this selfishness. Selfishness is an important process as described in previous chapters. It is not intended as a moral judgement. Inherently we all have slightly different DNA, and by definition we are therefore in competition. But this doesn't mean we ignore the rest of humanity and the living world. In order to survive, we rely on the support of our fellow man and the surrounding environment; therefore, it is vital that we take care of this situation even though it is for selfish reasons. Within that selfishness, however, can come a great ability to care and nurture.

Finally, it might be worthwhile noting a few observations concerning the differences in the male and female personality traits. The tripartite system appears to affect both males and females similarly, and as such, I have been unable to note any significant behavioural differences attributable to gender. The consequence of signal strength appeared similar as in the examples of Churchill and Thatcher. Differences in male and female behaviour appear to stem from specialisation within the brain initiated within the womb shortly after conception. I have read studies that suggest at birth some parts of the cerebellum were specialised to focus on language, sounds and spatial orientation and that females appeared to have better language ability and men better spatial orientation ability. This difference, I have since learned, was promoted in the womb when males could receive a greater amount of the hormone testosterone. In the time of cavemen, this difference would have had a distinct advantage. Apart from the obvious physical advantage, men needed spatial orientation for hunting. If he didn't, he wouldn't be able to hunt successfully for food, and the woman wouldn't want him. Consequently, this type of male would have no children and quickly become extinct. Spatial skills also required the male to concentrate on where the animal had been and where it might be in the future. As a result, males always seem to be dreaming about the future or thinking about the past, never about the present. The competitive and aggressive nature of males is also commonly attributed to testosterone, a feature that would have provided the assertiveness to defend the family and its related group.

The cave arrangement of the female brain appears to have been steered by other circumstances such as providing skills and abilities to suit her particular environment at that time. In contrast to the male, the female may have been left behind in the cave, possibly with her child or children and the other females that could have shared the same shelter. Her greatest concern would be the fear of being isolated, both within the cave community and from her hunting man. An instinct and understanding about the relationships ongoing around her would have been paramount. She needed to know what was going on right there and then at that time. She needed to be able to communicate, to have developed social skills and a cunning ability to keep her man bringing back the food to her and her children. In addition, she would have to be well organised, remembering where she had put the food and what state it was in. Today, females are often better than males at language, communication skills and organisation. Men, however, are usually (but not always) much better at map reading, understanding the importance of promptness and arriving on time, planning time schedules (the buffalo does not wait for the hunter if he's late). In our modern life, these inherent differences are less important, but they will probably remain as differences between men and women until a change is critical for survival.

Anger

Before we move on, there is one more fundamental emotion I have to consider within this set of dynamics, and that is 'anger'. It represents the opposite of happiness, but how did it fit into the parameters described above? There were various emotions that could fit into this category and could be related to the same mechanisms as anger. Irritation, for example, would appear to represent the mildest expression of anger. In my experience (at a young age), a feeling of irritation came after an expected pleasure was not received. For example, if I was able to obtain money from a cashier at a bank, I would feel a mild sensation of pleasure as I succeed in filling out the cheque correctly and receiving the 10-pound notes. The successful processing of the transaction increased my security, and I was allowed a mild rise in dopamine. However, if I made a mistake with the cheque and did not receive the pound notes, then my DNA via the tripartite system would feel temporarily stressed and instead instantly restrict my dopamine levels. As a result, I would feel mildly uncomfortable or irritated, especially since I was expecting to succeed and feel the consequent comfort of pleasure. Unfortunately, the brain observes the absence of money and perceives another equation that indicates a survival problem and, sensing insecurity, withdraws the pleasure. Should I fail two or three times more with the request, I would receive further restriction of dopamine if my expectation was to succeed. The increased discomfort leads on from irritation to frustration. The only way to relieve this anxiety is to perceive a new solution to the problem, that is, a new survival equation that will enable me to succeed. This way, DNA, again via the tripartite system has used the emotion of irritation and frustration to encourage me to find an alternative solution. Without this discomfort and the need to get the pleasure back, I would probably give up and do without.

If the problem continued on further, the threat of more discomfort might lead to anger, which could encourage me to find more extreme ways of resolving the equation. At such moments, I might be tempted to show my anger to achieve my goal. The cycle of escalating the restriction of dopamine represented here can be the same for any circumstance where the perceived survival equation is not achieved. Should the failure of the survival equation constantly increase the chance of personal danger, then obviously such cycles can lead to more violent solutions. Such escalating cycles can be contained by the greater threat of reprisal, whether it be immediate or longer term. The fine balance between escalation and the fear of reprisal would depend on inherent intelligence, experience and education. It also depends on one other very important factor which will be discussed shortly.

Another type of anger can be seen expressed by jealousy and envy. These emotions appear to perform the function of raising your awareness of a survival feature in someone else, which you do not possess and which presents itself to you as competition. DNA effectively lowers the influence of the opiate neurotransmitters each time you think about it and in this way prompts you to try and develop something better to counteract its competitive edge.

The Subconscious

All the brain cortex processes I had envisaged so far were being directed via the frontal lobe area, and as such, we would be very much aware of this activity within our conscious thinking. I strongly suspected, however, that there was circumstantial evidence to suggest that our reptilian brain still received and responded to information directly from the cortex without passing through the frontal lobe area. We would not be consciously aware of this activity since we didn't 'think' about it, and thus, the activity would be subconscious. The only time I could actually cross-check a part of this subconscious activity is illustrated in my earlier example with the 'fall'. In this case, as we fell, we actually received two sets of data about the incident. The sensory organs (not the frontal lobe) sent one set directly to the reptilian brain complex, which responded immediately to adjust our position. We did this without a survival equation and without knowing what we have just done. The other set of data would go through a longer process of comparing and assessing the situation from the frontal lobe with long-term memory. It would decide a low survival score and the need to adjust course. At this moment, we sensed fear and also confusion. We sensed confusion because we're now consciously aware of the 'falling' situation and that we had to adjust our position, only to discover that we had apparently already completed this adjustment. The earlier action was carried out by the automotive functions of the old reptilian brain and as such was a subconscious activity. I suspected that all activity that took place within this old reptilian brain area could be referred to as automotive and thus subconscious.

Esteem-Moral Conscience: Our Inner Policeman

Another concept to be considered in relation to subconscious activity is the possibility that the old reptilian brain might still continue to receive a limited amount of raw data directly from the cortex, especially since it appears to operate in the 'falling' example described above. The principle might exist since it seems the cortex initially evolved as an extension to the existing reptilian brain and that in earlier times received data directly, un-interpreted and un-summarised. It did not seem unreasonable to consider that a remnant of this former link still existed. The problem is that, should it really exist, the process would be subconscious and difficult to identify since it would not involve the frontal lobe area.

My interest in this possible route was aroused since it offered a possible explanation of experiences related to 'esteem'. The experience of high or low esteem seemed real, and at the same time vague, yet a difficult emotion to define. Again, within my own limited experience, it was not long-lasting but appeared at unusual moments, often against the prevailing tide of emotion at the time. For example, I could never really explain the varying levels of optimism or pessimism that I would experience as I stepped out my 'university digs' in the morning. Whilst I walked to college, there was very little to alter my mood, yet as I walked along, I occasionally experienced a sense of elation and optimism for no obvious reason. Equally I could be beset with a similar degree of pessimism. It would be normal to explain such elation as being related to the anticipation of something especially interesting in the days work ahead or that I had achieved something special the previous day and was feeling more confident. Similarly, uncomfortable experiences from the past could have sprung into mind to depress my mood. In practice, I had not been able to clearly identify these patterns. I could not support the idea that I had 'consciously' thought about any particular positive or negative thought prior to such moments of elation or depression. So if I was not consciously aware of the thoughts causing these swings, then it seemed more logical to consider the thoughts may have been 'subconscious'. If they were subconscious, how did these thoughts make their presence felt?

One explanation could be related to the possible direct link of the old reptilian brain to the cerebral cortex. If this link existed, it would mean that raw data from the brain cortex such as the long-term memory bank would be available. In addition, it's not impossible, although tentative, to envisage that all the 'old survival scores' created by the frontal lobe are stored within the cortex and that these would also be accessible. The reptilian brain would then have an opportunity to scan these 'old scores' and in this way could assess the current and general survival situation. It offered the reptilian brain a second cross-check of how things were going. This would be like checking your current bank account from time to time. The process would be carried out entirely at a subconscious level. If the balance seemed positive, then the reptilian brain would send a wave of pleasure just to encourage you to continue your current behavioural strategy since it appeared to be succeeding. The consequent elation would appear to come from nowhere and for no obvious reason just as in the experience described whilst leaving the digs. If the experience was elation, it promoted a feeling of well-being and higher esteem. As a consequence, you would have added confidence to move on.

If there was a wave of discomfort, it is likely that unpleasant memories of injustice or mistakes you had made in your social or business life were coming back to haunt you. This was essentially a part of your 'inner policeman' at work. Such memories cannot easily be removed and would remain as an unpleasant and sometimes distressing reminder. The fear of remorse returning would be an excellent survival strategy. It would encourage us to avoid mistakes of this type. It's tempting to believe evolution took full advantage of integrating this latent facility. Could it be that this is actually our 'moral conscience' at work?

Empathy

A not-so-rosy image of empathy is presented in the poem below.

> Empathy isn't generous,
> It's selfish. It's not being nice
> To say I would pay any price
> Not to be those who'd die to be us.

Figure 53.

Empathy can be the result and generated by several different sets of circumstances. The above poem is not the common view held by most people. However, it has always been my opinion that 'empathy' could be considered a selfish process. It is a survival tool, a social display.

In any interaction, we wish to communicate to others that we understand what they are feeling, especially in times of stress. An intense situation could be a threat to ourselves so we need to find a way to reduce this potential threat in others. For example, upon meeting someone new, it is common practice to ask what their interests are, what they enjoy and their general experiences. Where possible, we attempt to follow this by indicating where we might have similar areas of interest and experience. This is a mild show of empathy which we hope will form the basis for a benign, non-threatening interaction by indicating we, ourselves, do not present any threat.

Another way of ensuring this benign relationship could continue is to show our support in more stressful situations. We naturally tend to make facial expressions, body movements and even cry genuine tears that express support. Tears are known to be part of your lachrymal system (sac containing water) that sits next to your eyeballs. It is both a secretory system that produces your tears and an excretory system that drains them. They could clean the surface of the eye and prevent drying out, but they could also be discharged as a show of empathy within a sad, joyful or stressful situation. However, the process can actually be quite deceitful in the sense that we are putting on a show, an act, which in fact agrees with the sentiment declared in the poem above.

The degree of empathy is also dependant on the capacity of the person to visualise a sad situation. This can be similar to reading a sad story, whereby a new reality is created in the frontal cortex and the information sent along the tripartite system. As a consequence sadness of the imagined scenario can promote an uncomfortable and distressful feeling within ourselves. The more detailed this image becomes the deeper the display of empathy and the consequent distress. It can happen that the person trying to comfort a friend in distress also begins to cry. This process is also well illustrated when we watch a sad film. The story temporarily presents a new reality and we fight to hold back the tears.

Nevertheless, empathy provides a valuable tool that enhances our ability to survive amongst all the other competing DNA hosts (Figure 54).

Figure 54

14

LOVE AND ROMANCE

The genetic code must be passed on to younger, healthier hosts to carry DNA to ensure survival of organic life

Whilst looking into the brain and attempting to understand its functions, I was also examining the other survival condition we are striving to fulfil. As discussed earlier, it is equally important that the genetic code be passed on to an offspring to assure one's DNA that its future is secured and will continue in the succeeding generations. So whilst I, and my many university colleagues, went through and experienced the natural emotions of the mating process, I began to perceive the situations and emotions in the same unorthodox manner that I did survival.

College life provided a wealth of opportunity to meet the opposite sex and develop relationships. In my case, this potential was enhanced by the fact that my college had a few years earlier been for ladies only and was now sporting a ratio of 60:40 in favour of males. Despite this unparalleled start, I had not yet succeeded in finding a girlfriend.

Of course, many of the girls seemed unbelievably attractive. The hormones at this age were firmly established and doing their work. At times it felt uncontrollable. I'd have to calm myself. I would try sobering thoughts such as the potential threat of religious chastisement, physical deformity, famine, the plague . . . anything! It never worked. The very next girl that walked by started up the whole process again. Without doubt, girls were irresistible.

One such girl I met at a college 'Hop'. She was named Jane, blonde and shapely and, in the very low light of the dance floor, very attractive. I remember it well. The Hop was held in the college sitting room area but was not well attended. I had wandered in without having to pay and began to survey the scene. Jane stood with her back to the bar on the other side of the room, and I noticed her watch me as I made my way over to get a drink.

'Before you do that, would you like to dance?' she said without introduction. Of course I wasn't surprised at this. After all, I secretly held an innate belief that all girls found me irresistible despite what the mirror might say. It was only now, finally, after 18 years, of somehow managing to keep their distance, one of them had finally succumbed.

We danced. I felt clumsy and tried to moderate my dance movements. She seemed to sense my hesitation and pulled me closer to her. She was warm and friendly, and it felt good. It was much better than I'd expected. As we talked a little, it became obvious from her accent that she came from the South of England. Her manner was confident and reassured. This was my first close encounter with a lady from the South, a thought that suddenly made me acutely aware of my own Northern extraction.

Despite my misplaced confidence, I instinctively knew this situation was doomed. Her cultured accent strongly suggested her interest in me was going to be limited. Perhaps one dance, but then definitely the excuses would follow. Yet despite these reservations she did warm up to me. We seemed to enjoy the same sense of fun which I tried my best to provide. After all, without a sense of fun, what was there? She seemed a very distinguished young lady. Nevertheless, the fear of impending silence loomed uppermost in my mind, and I felt uncomfortable.

'Would you like to come to a party tomorrow night?' she asked. 'Some friends of mine are coming from home, but I still would like you to come.'

'I presume you mean your boyfriend when you say "friends from home"?' I said tentatively. I suddenly had visions of having to be terribly adult and sophisticated.

'Oh darling, you do make me smile,' she said conspicuously. The phrase rang out.

'Oh darling!' I repeated to myself.

The mere sound of it grated in my ear. I had no logical reason for this reaction, yet it jangled loudly. It was changing my perspective of her personality. Despite this, I was not going to let the situation go that easy. Somehow I put the pieces back together and tried to ignore it. She continued and explained the friends did include a boy she was quite friendly with but that she still would very much like it if I came. I accepted. It never really occurred to me to say no.

The party was the following night, held at a large but dilapidated flat near Queens Park underground station, for this was the way during that part of the sixties. I arrived by myself full of expectations. Any party was a rare event, and this one had the promise of excitement. The atmosphere was loud with anticipation. People were everywhere, huddled close in intimate conversation. Their posture suggested an urgency and intensity in what they had to say.

The house was an endless labyrinth of rooms and stairways. I eased my way past what seemed like a sea of strangers, recognising no one until I glimpsed Jane as I reached the third floor.

'My goodness,' I said to myself, taken a little by surprise, 'she is attractive.'

Two other gentlemen already engaged her in conversation. I stood nearby to listen and observe. The controlled nature of their conversation was impressive. As I drew closer, I could feel any attempt by me to speak was going to be an embarrassment. And so it was. My initial words sounded childlike and ineffectual in comparison. Jane acknowledged me with a smile and proceeded to introduce me to her friends. I remember thinking they looked quite different to the others at the party. They wore suits and had a hairstyle to match. They were clearly representative of the stockbroker belt, I decided. Not that I fully understood what a stockbroker really was in those days.

After the introductions, their discussions continued with the same authority and calm. The tone and syntax were totally alien to me. I'd only ever heard this kind of prose on BBC TV before. I stood there like a wallflower for a few minutes until a break in their conversation allowed Jane to lead me away to another part of the room.

Now I hadn't been to such a large gathering as this before, and as time passed, it slowly began to dawn on me that the party would go on all night and that Jane wanted me to stay. By now some people were beginning to leave, and others sat down around the edges of the room, leaving Jane and I still dancing.

My experience in such situations had never extended any further than this before, and I was becoming increasingly conscious of events possibly proceeding further. Without another word, Jane stood up and beckoned me into an adjacent room. It was a bedroom. Piles of coats had been strewn on the floor. In the murky light of the room, I could make out there were two couples in bed already. There was a third bed. We got into it fully clothed and cuddled a little more, but for some strange reason, I couldn't develop this any further. There I was, fully dressed and hesitating. We lay like this a long time. Despite everything, we were still relative strangers. In fact, I still didn't know her full name. But why was I thinking and not doing? This was an opportunity, the very first opportunity to do something my hormones had been thinking desperately about for years. The physical attraction was beyond dispute. The thinking continued until I eventually fell asleep.

In the cold light of the following day, I felt uncomfortable and embarrassed. The smell in the room was now distinctly acrid, and as I looked around everything seemed ugly and depressive. Even Jane didn't look so pretty anymore, and to my horror she sat up and removed her hair! It was a wig. The shock of this discovery depressed me even further. After a few awkward words, I left and made my way through the debris out into the morning air. It seemed clean, pure and refreshing, but inwardly I felt wretched and glad to have escaped.

Upon our next meeting, I was invited for coffee at her hall of residence at Swiss Cottage. We went upstairs to her room. She changed in front of me revealing without affectation her almost naked body. I was spellbound by this display. Surprised, I was uncertain how to react. There was no uncertainty of how my body had now, without my personal permission, transformed into a pulsating, lustful, wobbling jelly. I sat there locked in space, motionless, unable for some unfathomable reason to pursue a more lustful course as she brushed past me, leaning this way and that as she searched out her underwear. Everything seemed to be happening so quickly. At the same time, I suddenly noticed the wig sitting perched like an insect on the dressing table. I could have sworn it turned and winked at me. I looked elsewhere in the room for a distraction.

Before today, the female world had always been a closed door. Proximity of this kind I had not previously experienced. Except for the insect-like wig, it felt good. The show over, she sat at the dressing table to brush her hair – her real hair. I leaned over to give her a kiss. It seemed awkward, as I didn't really know her well enough. Yet it seemed perfectly in order for her to take her clothes off in front of me. Whatever the reason, nothing further happened. Every time I pursued the idea of making advances, there was nothing but foreboding appearing in my mind. It prevented any further development of the relationship.

At this stage, I couldn't really pinpoint the reason for my self-control. There was no lack of physical desire. Everything was working down below. It had crossed my mind that she might have some sort gruesome sexually transmittable disease, but I didn't really take this idea too seriously. I suddenly realised that this whole business was not as simple as it seemed.

'You don't look as though you've got a problem,' she said thoughtfully. We arrived back at the hall in Swiss Cottage. As I stood outside the car, Jane closed her door, paused and then leaned against the car.

'Mike,' she began. 'I do have another boyfriend. One of those chaps I was talking to yesterday evening.' I listened. 'I've known him a long time.' I waited for her to finish.

'He's actually my fiancé,' she said hesitantly, 'and we get married in September.'

For a moment I froze. I've never been interested in jewellery before, but now I found myself looking intently at her fingers. Sure enough there was the ring. Whether it had just appeared, I couldn't really say since I'd never looked before.

'So why this?' I said enquiringly, trying not to look hurt. A painful noise began to buzz in my head.

'Why did you want to . . .' I was starting to fluster.

'You're nice and I liked you,' she said softly. The words sounded warm and friendly, but I was in pain.

'I think it's that way to Kilburn,' I said in the same uncertain voice. I began to walk.

'Will you get back alright?' she called. I raised my arm in the air but didn't look back.

The walk home was tinged with regret but also relief. At least the rain had stopped and it was warm. I remember thinking why on earth I had put myself through this. From the moment we had met, my instincts have been telling me something was wrong – even that this was likely to happen. Instead of getting more morose about her, I tried to cheer myself up with the science of it all. Somewhere in here, biology was playing its full role.

'So what biologically was happening?' I said to myself.

I paused for a moment, and an image of Jane returned to torment my head.

'She was pretty.' I sighed. 'The DNA definitely approved – nothing wrong there. The genetic code would live on. So why wasn't it satisfied? Why couldn't it let me have a bit of fun?' I said frustratedly to the audience of passing cars. 'Why was it able to give me messages to the contrary? My brain could not know in advance she was already engaged. Or could it?' Despite my insistent tone, the cars wouldn't answer.

Clearly physical attraction alone was not sufficient to persuade the DNA to pass on the genetic code, although it obviously had a lot to do with the start of the whole process. I was surprised at the ability of the brain to send such frustratingly restraining messages when I was so emphatically within the grip of my pulsating and highly aroused jelly phase. Right at the very beginning, however, I did identify we were from contrasting backgrounds. This could lead to problems in the future, breakdown in the relationship, threats to care and continuity. Not a sound investment for the future survival of the super race of DNA.

No wonder it rang alarm bells. It would need much more information and reassurance before it would allow things to progress further. Without security in the relationship, the resulting children would be at risk. But it didn't receive those assurances. Several differences in our personalities were already beginning to show – possibly serious, possibly not. So despite the physical attraction, the brain via the tripartite system did all it could to dissuade me and protect my DNA. If I hadn't listened, the consequences would have been guilt and worry, a strong feeling of 'I wish I hadn't done that'. I was relieved to think that. It made more sense. In terms of DNA survival, personality did seem important after all.

The long-term memory remembering previous experience had an important role in assessing a suitable mate. It hurt the last time; therefore, it may remember not to do it next time. In this case, people who don't really get on with each other tend to split up. Having stated that, I didn't actually think that thought at the time we lay in bed together. I didn't carefully consider anything in particular when she was undressing in front of me, except of course the obvious. I just felt anxious and uncomfortable . . . and the more enjoyment I got from thinking about the obvious, the more anxious and uncomfortable I became. It is only afterwards when we concentrate and discuss the situation that these ideas and explanations come forward.

In effect, as I had demonstrated for our more everyday emotions, the overriding control remains within the reptilian brain. All this sophistication within the short- and long-term memories are there to provide the old reptilian brain with the best information possible prior to it allowing a particular course of action to be carried out. Our every single action, thought and sensory impulse is being monitored by the frontal cerebral cortex, where it's assessed for survival and then sent down to the old reptilian brain. And that's what stopped me taking a short-term action and receiving any dopamine or pleasure.

As you watched a potential partner walk and talk, the body's senses were detecting from the signals contained in the small movements of body language, signs of health and security. In the timing and pace of movement, in the pitch and modulation of the voice, are all the signs of cooperation, sincerity, devotion to duty and intellect that DNA via the tripartite system could monitor. It is looking for reliability and security, and it could use the very first few seconds of observation to decide this part of a suitable partner. Many of these features were not identified in my example with Jane. Despite my naivety and uncertainty, the brain had already decided. To register disapproval, it restricted the dopamine to bring about discomfort and unease. This way the brain hopes to discourage you from pursuing this potential partner further. However, in the case where it approves, it will send a wave of excess dopamine to encourage you to think more about this person. With each thought, you can receive more dopamine and consequently more pleasure.

So is there a classic, perfect partner that we can all fall in love with, or are most of us doomed to make the best of what is available? Will only a few be allowed to select and mate with the most beauty? Experience suggests that everybody has a different perception of the perfect partner.

There are classic features that signal all the necessary requirements for DNA, and that is why there are film stars that have universal appeal. As already discussed, there are certain universal ratios inherent in all organic life that will be detected and considered attractive by DNA. One of them is Leonardo da Vinci's golden ratio, discussed earlier, of approximately 1:3. Another is symmetry of facial features such as the eyes, nose and mouth. Organic structures appear to function at their optimum when they are placed adjacent to each other in these proportions. As a consequence, the face of a human contains a great number of these ratios within its features which enable it to demonstrate it is healthy to a potential partner. Such features, I believe, can be considered desirable and consequently attractive, often referred to as beautiful (Figures 40 and 55). To see your own asymmetries look at a photograph of your full face in a mirror.

However, DNA also wants security for the potential offspring carrying new DNA. It is looking for a partner that will form a stable relationship with you and your specific requirements. The most beautiful person in the world may not fit the criteria of stability. For example, despite Jane's clearly attractive features, my DNA focused on the potential instability, displayed from the first encounter. As soon as it heard the phraseology employed by Jane's ('Oh darling'), I felt the discomfort signal from the brain stem even though at the time I had no logical reason to be critical. In addition, should your beauty be of a lower standard, then this can be a threat to the stability of the relationship. Wedding photographs viewed in the local newspaper often show couples that look alike and are similar in their attractiveness. This provides a better basis for a stable relationship. Differences cause the eyes of DNA to wander and look for a better-proportioned specimen for its future vehicle. Again, I was aware of this difference with Jane and felt instinctively I would have to rely on my humour, as I did, to save the day.

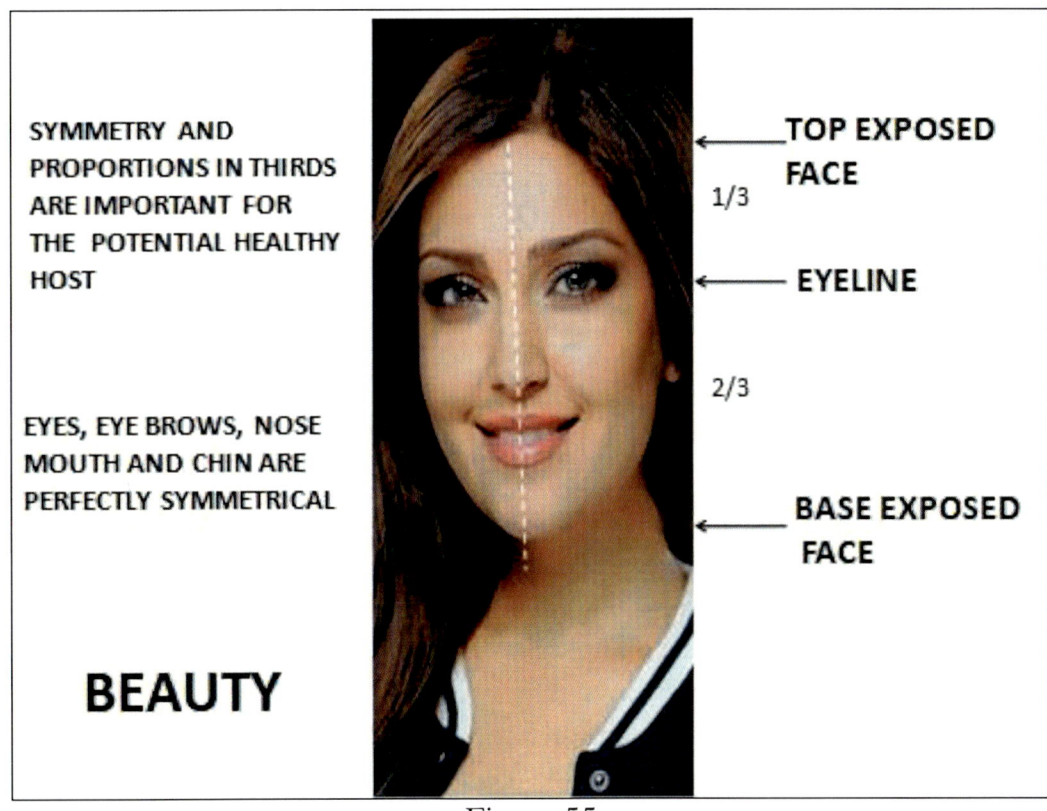

SYMMETRY AND PROPORTIONS IN THIRDS ARE IMPORTANT FOR THE POTENTIAL HEALTHY HOST

TOP EXPOSED FACE
1/3
EYELINE
2/3
BASE EXPOSED FACE

EYES, EYE BROWS, NOSE MOUTH AND CHIN ARE PERFECTLY SYMMETRICAL

BEAUTY

Figure 55

Having identified the partner is of a suitably balanced level of attractiveness relative to yourself, DNA, via the tripartite system, then concentrates on identifying specific features in the partner that suggest trustworthiness and reliability by selecting partners with features similar to a person you already trust. This could be a parent or even yourself. Many people marry a person who would look rather like themselves. Mistrust in oneself would lead you to choose someone quite different. Hence, the concept of beauty will vary enormously and be subject to these very individual and personal influences.

The frontal cortex could identify most of the essential features within a few seconds by the poise, timing, manner of walk, tone of voice and a host of other characteristics immediately upon meeting someone for the first time. For those people who meet their partner this way, it would be love at first sight. The frontal cortex will have made its decision whilst your brain is still thinking about the more mundane purpose of the meeting. Despite your more logical concerns to proceed with the meeting, you would become increasingly aware of a pleasurable and exciting feeling arising unexpectedly within. The feeling grows more intense as your gaze is being drawn more fixedly on this person. I still have a vivid memory of the first time I met my wife. As I watched her get out of her car and walk across a car park towards a restaurant, I experienced a very exciting and positive message. I felt the decision was made at that moment. The rest is Hollywood material.

Having steered your attention towards the selected partner, DNA, again via the tripartite system, then appears to activate a series of procedures to encourage and ensure your attentions continue. For example, your attempts to think about this person will be rewarded with a wave of pleasure. The more your mind is occupied with this person, the more you will experience the pleasure. So much so that your head becomes high with the amount of dopamine it receives. It encourages you to communicate words of bonding, promises of eternal care, activities that denote a future together. This process of tightening the bond also continues by stimulating small physiological changes that will enhance the pleasure derived from proximity and contact. For example, the pleasure derived from your partner's personal perfume is heightened such that upon meeting other females, you find their personal aroma of no interest and even unattractive. I always feel this is very conspicuous after I've been away from my wife for some time. On my return, the reunion with her personal perfume is a very comforting experience.
  Your DNA, via the tripartite system, also begins the transfer of some of

its survival focus onto the partner, allowing apparently 'unselfish' acts on behalf of the partner and not yourself. This is usually displayed by males when one gives up an opportunity to watch a vital football game because his fiancé asked him to accompany her to choose a wallpaper. However, it is actually still the selfish act of your DNA taking care of its potential future host. All this is rewarded with constant waves of pleasure (Figure 56). So much so that you would do almost anything for this person. You are now officially 'in love'.

LOVE

The ultimate most important survival equation for the DNA is the mating game. The successful mating with a partner that has the appropriate physical and mental attributes to produce and nurture a newborn HOST for the DNA will be rewarded with waves of pleasure via the Tripartite system supporting and urging you on.

This we call LOVE

Figure 56

As you progress in this elated state of happiness and pleasure caused by the opiates generated by this most important of security equations, your partner would still require further reassuring words, gestures and signs to confirm that you are still experiencing these waves of pleasure, that you are still genuinely in love with them and that you are still the correct partner for them. Words of love are essential but repetition of the same words and gestures at the same time and in the same situation is no guarantee that it is genuine. New information that supports this relationship security equation needs to be provided. The gestures do not need to be 'grand'. A touch, a compliment, a kiss that is unexpected can be exhilarating and reaffirms your 'love'. There may be times you receive pleasure from just hearing the sound of their voice or watching the way they move. Simply sharing your thoughts; these experiences can all inspire such moments. Planning trips or social events together, giving gifts, remembering birthdays, anniversaries all confirm the partner is in your thoughts. Sharing plans of future financial stability such as pension plans or a new business idea, show clear signs of continued commitment together. All of this can initiate, via the tripartite system, security for the DNA and pleasure for the 'host' (the partner). In other words, at various points throughout the entire relationship and as the years pass by, reassurances should always be communicated, and not left unsaid. In a relationship, it is no longer just your tripartite system and DNA that needs to feel secure, but also your partner's, too. Their, and thus your, happiness and contentment depend on it.

Jealousy and envy can become heightened during these times since the brain is constantly scanning the evolving romantic situation for potential threats to its continued development. A person who is perceived to have attractive qualities that could interest your partner would arouse insecurity, prompting lower levels of dopamine and making you feel uncomfortable, consequently arousing the emotions of envy and jealousy. You will not feel secure until it receives a survival equation that strongly suggests the competitive edge has been regained. This way, it prompts you to do something about your inadequacies and save the day.

The bad news is that, if you lose this potential partner, there are consequences. A lot of effort and evolution has been put into steering you and the potential partner towards the mating process. DNA had already packed its bags and was ready and waiting to move onto its bright new future host. But now she was gone; you had lost her. For the genetic code, this loss is a major tragedy. It is the single most important event in its entire existence. Its whole purpose and your purpose, as the host, is the safe transfer of the DNA genetic code into a healthy, carefully selected partner, to produce an offspring for future generations – and you failed. It is similar should a young child die. The emotional impact is devastating.

Retribution can be consequently severe. Immediately the dopamine would be severely restricted. It would not do this lightly. The drop would be dramatic and very uncomfortable, as though your body is being internally cut or beaten. Your mind would be in turmoil, as it would initially seek to find survival equations attempting to resolve the situation. But the only resolution is the return of the partner or child and so would not respond with any increase of dopamine. All other activities may receive the same treatment. Games, reading, places, friends, all the pastimes that once gave pleasure now do not generate anything. The restriction of dopamine is total. The prolonged mental discomfort of this denial could lead to depression and despair as the brain appears to give up trying (Figure 57). Songs have been sung, poems written and endless films made describing this moment. It is an experience most humans never forget.

OUR MORAL CONSCIENCE AND INNER POLICEMAN

There is no escape from the withdrawal of dopamine and the anxiety and pain it causes. Acts as our moral conscience, our Inner Policeman. It delivers this punishing experience if we fail to balance the Survival Equation by restricting our natural opiates, such as dopamine at the synaptic gates.

Figure 57

It takes time to find a suitable replacement for a suitable partner. The blueprint of the previous partner is engraved in the system. Any new offerings will have difficulty being recognised. It seems reasonable to assume this blueprint would have to fade in order for the process to begin anew. At this stage, the dopamine might slowly return.

But let's return to happier days. The partner is still with us, and DNA continues steering you towards its ultimate requirement: the generation of a new host to carry the genetic code onwards. Once assured of stability, it gives you ideas via proximity, touch and rhythms to entice you into the reproductive act. Even during the act, it allows further, more intense signals of erotica, combined with dopamine, that make it almost impossible to stop until climax has been reached and the process completed. Nature via DNA leaves nothing to chance. In the natural world, there are no instruction books, no diagrams or advice centres.

Immediately after climax, it appears that the DNA switches off the dopamine for the man, who immediately loses interest. This is probably done deliberately to persuade the male to return back to security duty since there is now a possible new host being generated. The female is encouraged to remain calm and motionless to allow fertilisation.

DNA also appears to be sufficiently influential and able to send signals that will attempt to suppress a liaison from entering into any form of sexual action if there are doubts (as with Jane). This might usually happen when the longer-term consequences of this new relationship have not been established, or there is some obvious problem from the outset. In these cases, the physical desires may not be allowed to be consummated because of the strength of doubts surrounding the situation.

It might appear that the drive of the DNA to secure the transfer of the genetic code to future generations would lead individuals, especially males, to mate with as many different partners as possible, a veritable orgy of desire for the opposite sex. This desire does, in principle, appear to exist. Our early liaisons often attempt to sustain more than one relationship at the same time. The more attractive you are, the more this desire can activate promiscuous and flirtatious social activity. Experience shows, however, that when a focus has been established on a particular partner, the partner immediately requires signals of security and stability. Having more than one partner would seriously undermine the ability to be able to offer this future security. Once there is a suspicion that there are other partners, it senses future children may not be guaranteed the best available care and attention; their future may be compromised. Suspicion and doubt begin to plague the relationship or relationships. It would be almost impossible to sustain a close loving relationship in such an environment of concern. In our Western world, this concern is exacerbated by the moral codes of our society. These codes attempt to enforce security by encouraging monogamous relationships and marriages. Exceptions to this trend appear where imbalances within the society oblige other solutions. The tiny populations on some of the small Pacific islands, for example, especially when suffering from a shortage of suitable males, can actively encourage and accept carefully monitored bigamous and polygamous marriages. Such arrangements can serve the interests of the DNA better.

A final comment is that the experience of 'love' in its fullest form is not experienced by everyone. There are no statistics on such an opinion, but it seems safe to say that less than 50 percent of relationships are more based upon practical advantages than their loving nature. Indeed, as is well-known, some relationships can suffer from differences in the depth of feeling enjoyed by each partner. For example, those deeply in love can be manipulated and used by a partner less committed. However, when trust is achieved, it appears the DNA system is capable of persuading each of the partners to accept less attractive functions.

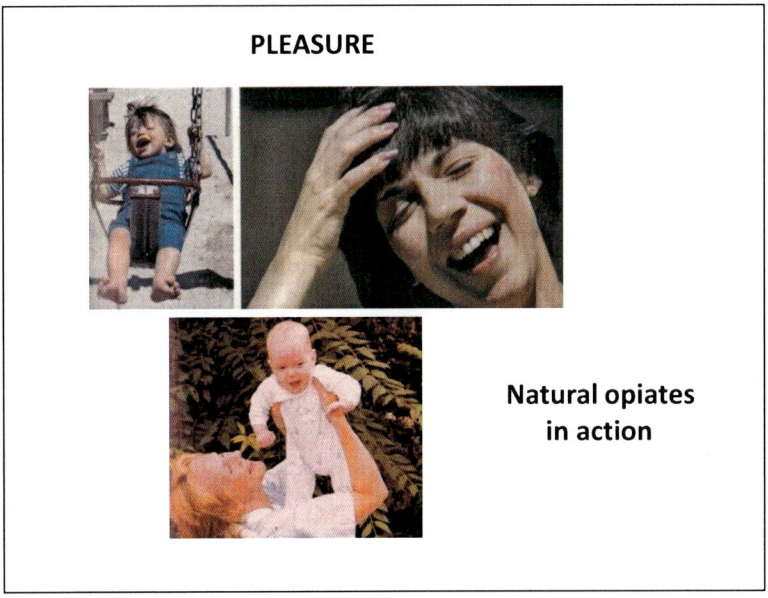

Figure 58

For most couples, the relationship is surrounded by a feeling of serenity, as DNA continues to urge care and concern over the imminent offspring during pregnancy. When the baby finally arrives, DNA is thrilled at the successful transfer of the genetic code onto a new host and congratulates all concerned with an abundance of joy (Figure 58). Both parents will be filled with pride at the sight of this achievement.

Their previously monogamous lifestyle will now hold little interest. Almost magically, their primary concern is child welfare. Aspects about the outside environment previously considered fun may now be actively avoided. Stable relationships with neighbours and the community become more important. We call this 'growing up', but it is actually the genetic code of the DNA steering us by its careful control of the opiate neurotransmitters to focus on its requirements.

In the photograph shown in Figure 58, the glow of joy displayed by the mother holding the baby up high for all to see is really the frontal cortex assessing that this vision has massive survival value and signalling the brain stem to provide a high surge of dopamine. The genetic code of the DNA has passed successfully on to a healthy and vibrant new generation. At last, the ultimate goal of the *Life Force* has been satisfied.

15

SIGMUND FREUD

At the time of writing, there was very little literature describing human behaviour and their controls. The exception was Sigmund Freud. He was fascinated by the influence of our subconscious.

The 'subconscious' activities I have referred to all involve the old reptilian brain area. This is a little different from the subconscious activity described by Sigmund Freud (Figure 59). Freud describes a process in which the frontal lobe area blocks out unwanted survival scenarios being constructed and prevents unwanted memories from the cortex entering the equation. This process could indeed be envisaged as a part of the activities learned by the frontal lobe. Once a particular association of memories or construction is recognised as regularly creating a low survival score and pain, it seems logical the brain will attempt to select out these features, especially if the memory provides no consequence for immediate survival. Since the neural network is so complex, it is difficult to block it out entirely since the offending memory may be tied to so many other, more innocent data points within the long-term memory of the brain.

We all carry around memories of bad experiences we would rather forget. As described by Freud, from time to time they will reappear, subtly attached to other less malevolent constructions, as slips in phraseology (Freudian slips), stressed behaviour and within our dreams. Unfortunately, as we get older, the list of bad experiences can only get larger and burdensome. It appears that the brain's rather effective survival system has no natural built-in mechanism to deal with this apparently pollutant baggage of redundant bad memories and has to rely, instead, on this improvised blocking process. This so-called pollutant baggage, however, is an integral part of our 'inner policeman'. As described earlier, we can never forget our transgressions that could threaten the survival of our DNA. It is there to discourage any repetition of such behaviour.

Whilst on the subject of Freud, this might be an apt moment to comment on how some of his other basic concepts compare with the alternative DNA-dominated steering process proposed in this book. Freud essentially proposes three basic personality systems: the *id*, the *ego* and the *superego*. Each system has its own functions, but the three interact to govern behaviour (Freud, 1923).

Figure 59

The *id* is considered to be the most primitive part of the personality, from which the *ego* and the *superego* later develop. It is present in the newborn infant and consists of the basic biological impulses (or drives): the need to eat, to drink, to eliminate wastes, to avoid pain, to gain sexual pleasure and to express aggression. The *id* is believed to seek immediate gratification, like a child, regardless of external circumstances. This description appears to compare very closely to what we now know about the functions of the old reptilian brain and the immediate demands and requirements of DNA, as presently described. It is essentially a picture of the old reptilian brain function.

The *ego* is said to obey the 'reality principle', and the gratification of the above impulses must be delayed until the appropriate environmental conditions are found. It decides what actions are appropriate and which *id* impulses will be satisfied and in what manner within the realities of the world.

The *superego* is essentially the individual's conscience. It decides whether an action is right or wrong within the values and morals of the society we live in.

Both the ego and the superego appear to fall within the context of the survival equation. We are all in competition with each other and to survive we sometimes have to assert ourselves in order to protect our security. It often manifests itself as aggression (*ego*). The degree of aggression and our behaviour will be assessed from previous experience of these circumstances, provided by the subtle interaction of the long term memory (*super ego*), and the current situation being observed by the frontal lobe. The survival threat will then be relayed down to the old reptilian brain (*the id*) which may signal restriction of dopamine and the addition of adrenaline. The consequent discomfort and tension you feel can provoke harsh and angry words and even an eventual physical attack.

In other words, much of what Freud describes does in fact conform to the premise of this book. The present philosophy, however, places his observations within a more scientific and understandable context.

16

DISTORTIONS OF THE TRIPARTITE SYSTEM

As with the work of Freud, any discussion regarding the brain was not really complete without some reference to mental illness and other commonly experienced psychiatric ailments. I had seen how the brain's activity could be controlled by the tripartite system of the frontal lobe, the old reptilian brain and opiate neurotransmitters. It appeared to be a fully integrated and self-sustaining system. So I wondered how the introduction of drugs, alcohol and malfunctions might distort the system and the balance within the brain.

For example, if we drank too much alcohol, this appears to have the effect of raising the lower survival scores so that we can feel happy and optimistic. The strong signal would be inhibited by the alcohol and temporarily create a weaker signal. Imagine that the ideal balance line '5' shown in Figure 44 would gradually rise to '4' or '3'. So with alcohol, this previously nervous introverted person could start behaving like a jovial extravert no matter the actual survival value of the thought. In such a situation, we could do the craziest of things, including putting the body at risk, completely convinced it was okay because we would be feeling happy. When the effects of the alcohol wear off and the stronger signal returns, we would feel not only the physical pain of dehydration but also the discomfort of the returning memories of all the low-scoring actions we had carried out under these impaired conditions. This heightened level of self-criticism, our **inner policeman**, would be quite uncomfortable, as the dopamine was restricted, a reminder against repeating the experience.

Mental illness can result from the impairment of a myriad of functions within the brain. Despite this, the survival equation of the tripartite system would probably still attempt to operate, and thus it would be useful to quickly consider the effects. For example, I observed several types of mental illness related to post-natal depression, affected disorder, depression, hyper-manic depression and schizophrenia. All these illnesses can be very distressing not only for the sufferer but also those trying to cope and understand the situation.

In my limited experience, I would tend to distinguish 'depression' more as a disorder of signal strength. If signal strength increased, negative life experiences could become exaggerated. For example, it is usual practice for people to acknowledge each other as they pass by – a smile or a 'nod' or even just a glance. When this acknowledgment is repeatedly lacking, DNA, via the tripartite system, might immediately detect a problem and a possibility of being isolated and excommunicated from society. A failure in your approach is suspected by the repeated negative survival equations it receives. To alert you to this possibility, the tripartite system arranges a lowering of support from the opiate neurotransmitters, causing a general feeling of discomfort and insecurity in an attempt to bring about a change in your social strategy. As described earlier, this would include a general reduction to our background contentment. If the new strategy is not successful and new, more optimistic survival equations are not received, this exaggerated negative feeling of discomfort is continued to the extent that the person may experience a loss of esteem and confidence and possibly develop depression.

Another more severe form of depression can be experienced by mothers immediately after childbirth. It would seem post-natal depression is more likely to appear in the mother after the birth of her first child since the physical experience of giving birth may have been severe and frightening, causing extreme panic. In such a case, the reptilian brain would have received messages of extreme fear and physical pain. The tripartite systems would interpret this situation as life-threatening and begin a series of self-defence processes that would help to protect itself. As with animals that are threatened, they retreat by shutting down all essential bodily functions and cower in a corner. When a human being is suddenly placed before a hungry wild bear, it faces two alternatives. As described earlier, the first is a massive amount of adrenaline being released to prepare you to flee from the situation. In case that this is not possible, the body is immobilised, freezing you on the spot. This way, it is hoped, as a last-ditch effort, that their stillness and inactivity will elude the predator. Perhaps it would be similar with the post-natal form of depression in that restriction of dopamine and adrenaline reduces the ability of the body to take action and renders the mother almost immobile. The consequent loss of motivation experienced by the mother results in depression. Only when the tripartite system is convinced circumstances have returned to normal would the dopamine reward return.

Hyper-manic depression can be cyclic, with each cycle lasting 2–4 months. It affects both men and women although women are most at risk. The illness may begin with indications of disorientation. Very early indications can be excessive use of descriptive terminology, odd statements said out of context with the situation. Sometimes obsessive rearrangement of paperwork, furniture, clothes. Such features are suggestive that the area of concentration that determines the logical thinking process is malfunctioning. It is clearly not able to sort out the order of events.

Gradually the language becomes more fanciful and imaginative. Images of royalty paying the individual visits, spies being placed all around them, are examples. Eventually their actions become more odd and outrageous as paranoia develops. Attempting to resolve the situation, the person may attempt to seek refuge by 'escaping' and can disappear without warning to visit a sunny holiday resort, see an old acquaintance or visit loud music shows. None of these bring any satisfaction because they are unable to concentrate on what is really happening around them. The frontal lobe is unable to process the incoming data logically. They are only able to say peculiarly arranged sentences which focus more and more on their own immediate personal needs.

Their tone can become demanding and urgent and their behaviour increasingly hyperactive. In this disturbed condition, adrenaline may be generated as the brain receives more and more messages of distress and fear. Often there is an inability to tell the time. They can see the clock but cannot interpret it. On one occasion, an individual went searching for bigger and bigger clocks in a desperate attempt to solve the problem. Unfortunately, there was no improvement, so after attempting to take the clock to pieces, it was placed in the refrigerator to get better. They are only vaguely aware of their confused behaviour and activities.

One other feature is the increasing pleasure followed by the stress they endure. The pleasure can be seen to gradually rise in waves within them, to the level of euphoria. At this stage, it appears that the 'loop' of dopamine reward for high survival scores, described above, may have continued excessively, not tempered by sufficient self-criticism. The person can display a very self-confident, even amorous, persona during this stage, totally convincing strangers who are unaware of the situation. All this suggests that despite their inability to concentrate properly, they are able to construct imagined high-scoring survival equations. Perhaps, as with alcohol, the survival bar has lowered. As a consequence, the dopamine loop grows. Equally the imagined scenes need not be at all positive; they can be unrealistic and distressful. Perhaps again the survival bar has moved, only this time higher. Such imaginations may then frighten and bring them to strike out and scream with rage. Left unchecked, this constant excessive emotional turmoil exacerbated by amounts of adrenaline (due to their disoriented state of mind and inability of the frontal lobe to resolve the situation) exhausts the individual, and they would slip into an extended period of depression. As the survival bar returns to its normal position, logical functioning makes a return. The depression, however, is now compounded by remorse, as the consequences of their previous behaviour is remembered and dopamine and adrenaline are withdrawn. Unfortunately, normal thought processes appear to remain only for a short period. After a month or two, the symptoms begin to reappear. It is the initial disorientation and lack of ability to rationalise correctly that appear to trigger the cycle.

The actual origins of the initial disorientation causing hyper-manic depression remain a mystery. It often first manifests itself in the late teenage years after the individual has left home for the first time and experiences new pressures. Some recent work suggest it is a degenerative disease.

With these examples, I hoped to illustrate how mental illness could be perceived in terms of the survival equation and the tripartite brain dynamics. Again, the relationship between the evolving cortex and the old reptilian brain complex appears to be a key to the way we function. Based on this relationship, it is possible to understand more and more about some of our more everyday emotional experiences and their controlling mechanisms.

However, there are other more subtle distortions of the brain that can affect the DNA's perception of the outside world and consequently our survival. For example if we are raised within an isolated environment where violence is an expected and normal response to achieve our goals and survival, the DNA will accept and reward this behaviour via the tripartite system. This isolated environment can be limited to a family unit or the culture and behavioural norms of a nation. Importantly, this norm can be manipulated. It is a similar process to that described earlier for games and story-telling. By suspending reality, the rules of engagement can be changed. Hence in isolation, without further information, a new reality can be all too easily imposed. A violent parent or national leader employs this isolation to impose their destructive doctrines such that other members of the family or the people of that nation will follow. This change in attitude and behaviour can spread like a virus. A prime example is the part played by Hitler, the leader of the German nation at that time, during the nineteen-thirties, where he turned peaceful methods of reviving a failing economic recovery to violence and war. Communication at this time was limited to the nation's radio, cinematic films and local newspapers. They could all be controlled and manipulated. Their media focused on strength, that is physical strength, and that this was paramount to their future success. Even Darwinism and the Survival of the Fittest was inaccurately employed as scientific proof to support the Hitler philosophy. Cultural attitudes were slowly changed to accept violent methods to obtain the required resources to sustain their success and survival. Even within their own small communities the population was encouraged to extricate individuals (often violently) that they considered unsuitable or hindered their march towards economic recovery. In this isolated situation they were not exposed to world opinion which might have tempered this acceptance of violence. As a consequence their DNA received positive messages, in association with violence, and improving security and survival. This only served to encourage this 'negative' behavioural attitude.

In stark contrast, today's attitudes have changed due to the improvement in communications worldwide. Violence is no longer high on the menu. 'Peace and love' 'human rights' have become the national cry across most democratic societies. More recently, tolerance of violent and abusive behaviour, at all levels in society is becoming unacceptable. This more positive attitude has a high survival value for us all and is readily accepted and rewarded by the DNA. Obviously, we all hope this will continue.

In summary, control and manipulation of information received by our senses, both at a local, national and even worldwide scale can have a powerful impact on the response of our DNA. When this information is deliberately steered and focussed to an isolated audience there will be a similar 'collective' response. Dependant on the nature of the information it could be a collective positive or negative result. Beware therefore, who it is that controls and influences the information we receive.

17

ORIGINS OF LIFE ON EARTH

Are we home-grown here on Earth or seeded from elsewhere in the Universe?

Having discovered that organic life has a role to play in the survival of the Universe, I pondered this constant attachment to DNA desires to continue the future of organic life. We seemed to endure a lot for this distant future, a future that we would never get to see, constrained and controlled by the rollercoaster ride of dopamine. I began to ask myself, *Could we still guarantee the survival of organic life without it?* Perhaps there is a way we can take more control and extract a longer and more pleasurable life.

But the reality is we could never rid ourselves of this control imparted by DNA and the tripartite system. Without this, life as we know it would collapse. This principle is fundamental to our continuation. There is no alternative. We seem doomed to spend our whole lives performing survival equations to receive the reward of a few morsels of happiness. Or, if viewed from another perspective, we are destined to be eternal entrepreneurs. We must always be trying to set new goals and achieving new targets to receive our moments of happiness.

The conclusion seems bleak. Our DNA was too powerful. But where did such DNA come from? Did it really spontaneously evolve within the muds of the primordial seas? Was it really a fortuitous combination of chemicals statistically inevitable in the processes of time, or could it have had another origin? When thought about this way, it raises a few questions.

For example, it seemed strange to me that there appeared to be only one system of life, that is, one system based on DNA. There is no other form or structural arrangement that remotely approaches something we would refer to as 'living'. Crystal structures organise themselves in very orderly ways, but the arrangements, although sometimes beautiful to look at, are actually very simple. Life, by contrast, is very complex and ordered in a very precise manner. The simplest form of life requires millions of parts at the atomic level. The macromolecules making up the cell organelles, essential for the cell to function, possess infinitely complex structures. This is especially illustrated by the sophisticated structure of DNA (as it exists today) and its surrounding living cells.

No other form we have so far encountered in the Universe remotely approaches the unbelievable complexity of this arrangement we simply refer to as 'life', and life could not exist without the pre-coded blueprint provided by DNA. It is this vital ingredient, and only this ingredient, that has been able to produce living systems. All other attempts both in the natural world and in the scientific world (at the time this manuscript was written) have failed to reproduce, imitate or artificially create this condition we call 'life'. There is an enormous leap from the synthesis of basic organic chemicals to the creation of a fully functioning, self-sufficient, fully reproducing living cell.

STANLEY MILLERS EXPERIMENT

Figure 60

The famous examples of Stanley Miller (Figure 60), who, during his research, worked for Harold Urey, attempted to recreate within his laboratory the conditions thought to have prevailed immediately prior to life beginnings.

In this experiment, they filled a sealed glass with methane, hydrogen, water vapour and ammonia, representing what they believed to be the composition of the Earth's atmosphere and seas at that time. To simulate lightning, they employed a spark discharge device. The experiment apparently yielded 10 of the 20 amino acids required for life. Although this result provided some evidence that the basic building blocks for life could be spontaneously generated here on Earth from inorganic substances, there remained problematic questions. The experiment yielded equal quantities of both right- and left-handed molecular forms whereas in natural life, nearly all amino acids found in proteins are left-handed forms. A misplaced amino acid type can be toxic to a living cell.

Yet another problem is that despite the ability to generate these basic building blocks, the question remained as to how they combined in such a complex manner to form a living organism. Several recent discoveries have led to the suggestion that life may have originated close to submarine volcanic vents. Here, temperatures may reach in the order of 350 degrees Celsius, which would help explain, perhaps, why some of the oldest known organisms required warm temperatures of around 80–110 degrees Celsius (Levy and Miller, 1998). In addition, the early Earth's temperature was believed to be much higher than it is today because of the greenhouse effects of the atmosphere at that time. Unfortunately, some of the most important molecules, such as adenine, uracil, guanine and cytosine, will break down too fast in a warm environment. In other words, these fundamental molecules were too unstable and wouldn't be around long enough and in sufficient numbers for random processes to act in favour of construction. Degradation would be pre-eminent. The problem thus remains how to assemble and correctly order sufficient quantities of the fundamental molecules to build by chance the highly sophisticated and precise mechanism of life.

Clearly the magical appearance of RNA and DNA, approximately 3–4 billion years ago, changed the face of this planet. This perfectly organised molecular structure, a miniature copying machine, sits in stark contrast to the relative simplicity of its constituent parts. The ingredients (sugars, phosphates, nitrates and so on) lay in abundance all around us, just like you could step into any supermarket and find all the ingredients for a cake. Yet, as far as we know, none of these ingredients are able to organise themselves into a self-replicating molecule, just as the eggs, milk and sugar cannot spontaneously make a cake. To make a cake, you need a recipe and a cook. There is a big leap from these basic structures to a fully functioning self-replicating molecule or even small slice of cake. This leap becomes even greater in an attempt to imagine how these constituents could randomly assemble themselves into a cell complete with the required fully functioning components and biochemical systems.

The only other way to envisage this happening is to have sufficient time, that is, to leave the ingredients of the supermarket alone for billions of years to mix randomly together and wait for a chance to come up with the correct recipe or order to make a cake. This is not a totally impossible scenario except that statistical experiments, so far, have tended to suggest there hasn't been enough time to evolve all the chemical stages required to build the complex molecular structure of the first cell with an inbuilt reproductive system. Estimates of 1 in 10 to the power of 119,879 have been suggested for the time required to randomly generate proteins needed to build a cell. This amounts to 4.5 billion years. It would still require more time to evolve the constituent organelles and membranous structures. Without all these stages in place at the same time, the system would degrade and be destroyed. It is indeed a strange conundrum.

Palaeontology suggests evolution took place gradually but sometimes irregularly. Having spent a major part of my career as a palynologist and geologist, I have been able to observe evolutionary mechanisms in detail (Whitaker, 1984; Whitaker et al., 1992). In my particular specialty, where I study the morphologies of cysts from planktonic organisms (dinoflagellate cysts), it is possible to observe the gradual evolution of their cysts with all the intermediate stages fully represented prior to a particular event. However, evolutionary boundaries can be blurred by external factors such as climate change or cratonic plate movements. Quite often, for example, a particular form well suited to a particular environment may flourish in vast numbers, which then suddenly vanish when the environment changes. New forms that were previously sparse or even absent may suddenly flourish when a suitable environment reappears. Their sudden appearances and disappearances are sometimes interpreted as an inception or extinction event. Usually, these events are related to sea-level changes, which may introduce migration of forms from outside the area after sea levels rise or massive deaths when sea levels fall and the sea becomes restricted. Falling sea levels can cause blooms, and then suffocation and mass deaths, because of lack of oxygen. Without close inspection, these events may give the impression that new forms have suddenly appeared or become extinct. These apparent gaps in development can almost give the appearance of spontaneous evolution.

Another example, this time from the world of larger vertebrate fossils, also shows this feature of an apparent gap in evolution without intermediates. As described earlier, a few small primitive mammals were already evolving and developing in the Late Cretaceous period, some 70–100 million years ago, but their presence was subdued by the numbers and dominance of the reptiles at this time. A complete change in environment imposed by the now-famous meteorite impact at the end of the Cretaceous period 60 million years ago, however, allowed the mammals the opportunity to flourish.

Employing these latter examples, couldn't it be that the highly specialised nature of the DNA molecule also suggests a long and maturing development elsewhere, somewhere where there was more time and more chance? Could it be, perhaps, that DNA evolved first within a stellar system within our galaxy some billions of years earlier where the environment was more suitable? This way, there was more time and perhaps more suitable pathways available for the required chemical evolution.

If this was possible, perhaps there is an alternative explanation to the origin of life. For example, perhaps DNA was seeded in a partial or completed form from outer space. This was not an entirely new concept. As discussed, Fred Hoyle, the eminent British scientist working with carbon remains, including amino acids, found in meteorite material, had suggested that viruses may have been transported by ice locked inside comet rock material. NASA has recently found evidence that cell membrane tissue may have been seeded from space. Employing these concepts, could we suggest that DNA evolved earlier, somewhere else in outer space, perhaps within our galaxy (Figure 61)? Isn't it reasonable to assume that we are also intimately involved with the environments that surround us in the cosmos?

Figure 61

Could it be that the DNA presents some sort of advanced form of parasitic virus surviving from a stellar explosion billions of years ago, preserved in ice and carried by comets across space to our planet? Could we also suggest that this advanced form of virus carried a code, a unique replicating system that would enable it to absorb and employ the available elements to build its own host and therefore guarantee its eventual survival? What better way for life to be transported over the vast periods of space and time within the cosmos, yet another example of the *Universal Life Force* at work. This way, the elements of the previous time-consuming evolutionary work of chance reactions and constructions are avoided. The replication system might arrive here on earth preserved complete with parts or even with complete sequential information of how to build a host organism. This primitive virus-like form has the ideal characteristics of being able to construct any form of life suitable for the particular planetary conditions into which it lands. It will be flexible and able to adapt quickly to the constituents available.

On some planets, it builds organic blobs; on another, it builds little green me; and on this planet, it builds a vast diversity of forms from simple cells, to plants, to insects, to humans.

The idea improves when you consider that parasites outnumber all other forms of life. They live in billions intimately associated with all organic matter and even our body, both outside and inside. Figure 62 shows the pyramidal structure of living forms traditionally shown in learning sets provided for teaching.

ENERGY FOOD CHAIN

NOT ALL ENERGY PASSED ON

THUS PYRAMID REPRESENTS A REDUCTION OF ALL AVAILABLE ENERGY AS WELL AS POPULATION

ENERGY

CARNIVORS

HERBIVORES

PLANTS AND PHYTOPLANKTON

CARNIVORES CONSUME HERBIVORES

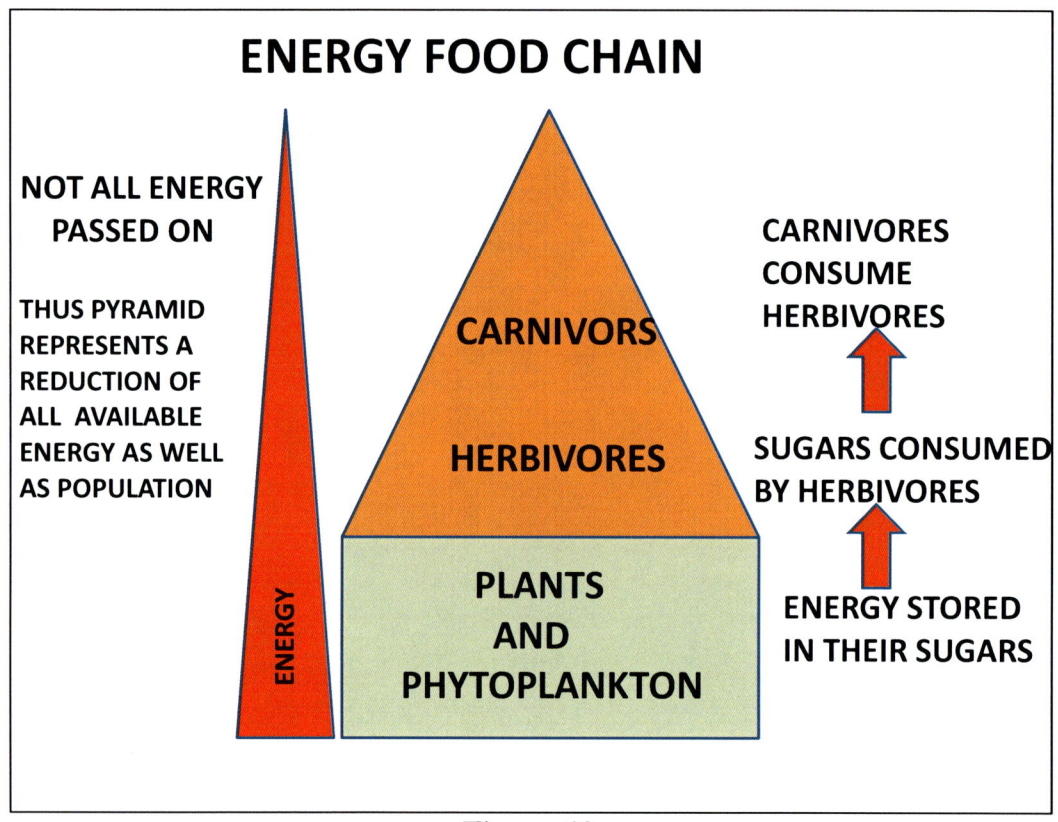

SUGARS CONSUMED BY HERBIVORES

ENERGY STORED IN THEIR SUGARS

Figure 62

It carries the implication that plant life dominates, followed by the herbivores, carnivores and then ourselves. This is an unintended misconception the diagram portrays yet one that many students take with them.

The reality is that parasites are the most abundant life form and that this diagram should be modified and expanded as shown in Figure 63. This way, the parasitic lifestyle can be viewed as the norm, not the exception. It is the most potent and virulent known life form.

PARASITIC LIFE VERSES NON PARASITIC LIFE

PARASITES and other microbes

Carnivores

Herbivores

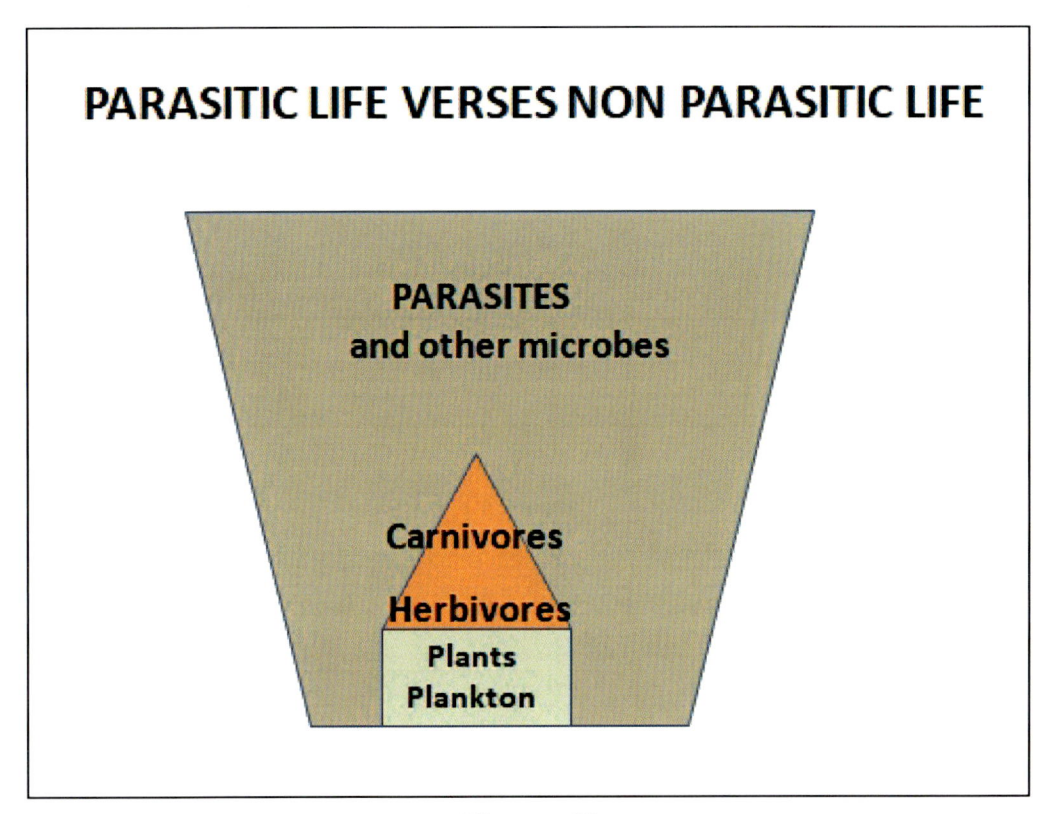

Plants
Plankton

Figure 63

Having proposed that DNA may have been seeded in this parasitic form from outer space, there are still some practical physical constraints to consider. Can such organic fragments survive the transit time in space and the transition into the Earth's atmosphere without being totally destroyed? The friction and heat generated as comet ice and rock pass into the denser atmosphere and the intense explosions on impact with the ground are not easy to overcome without considerable damage. The answer to this, I believe, lay in the precise nature of the atmosphere at the time and the size and abundance of the ice particles, and we know that both these factors varied. However, in support of the seeding hypothesis, it is believed there were periods when unusually high inputs of ice from outer space may have sourced the water of our primordial seas, thus raising the statistical chance of some alien RNA-DNA surviving entry.

Given time, we have seen it is possible to evolve a multi-purpose human host able to provide the security and technical abilities to survive. DNA is a replicating machine, an advanced virus, and as we have discussed in earlier chapters, it can build its own host cells from the available materials.

Considered this way, the human being appears not an independent life form since the outer cellular content acts as a host for the inner RNA-DNA nucleus, a parasitic virus which, in reality, controls everything. It appears we must conform and are thus subservient to the requirements of DNA. It guarantees survival via the tripartite system, which employs the supply and restriction of drugs (natural opiates) to control our behaviour. We do this blindly, without knowledge of its existence. If this is true, our happiness depends on it.

But it doesn't stop there. DNA goes on to permeate our entire social structure. Its desire for security is insatiable.

18

EXTENDED FAMILY OF DNA

Community and social structures

After securing the health of the host and offspring (as discussed in previous chapters), DNA could steer the host to secure sustenance for the extended family and to build a protection around them against the threat of an ever-changing outside environment. I suspect it does this by exciting our creative thinking. It develops via the tripartite system the concept of 'ideas' created and rationalised within the prefrontal cortex as an extension of the survival equation, enabling DNA by approval to manipulate and order our surrounding environment.

Employing this process would encourage the idea of shared cooperation with benign competitors. However, such a system may carry risks. Some competitors would seek to dominate or destroy their competition in an attempt to secure their own survival. By establishing a cooperative pyramid, however, each competing contributor receives a shared benefit but at the same time is tied inextricably into the system such that the benefits are greater than the deficits. This way, the threat of the competitor is reduced. It is not in the interests of the contributors to rock the boat. Their own survival would be threatened. Consequently the 'idea' created within the prefrontal lobe is approved and encouraged by raising dopamine levels.

Another example of benign cooperation is illustrated by a farmer who has gained enough land that he requires the help of others to work his fields. This way, he secures more produce for sale whilst at the same time eliciting the cooperation of his potential competitors. Their potential threat is made benign because they are dependent on his sales.

This passive co-existence with otherwise threatening competition is sustained by the continual growth of the pyramid and the increased security and benefits it offers. Such growth can be represented by the small businesses and factory-scale cooperatives that exist in our societies today. The pyramid is allowed to grow through the increasing specialisation of the front end as represented by the increasing diversity of available services and products. Here, individuals and groups cooperate to produce security for those higher in the pyramid. They do this with the motivation that they too will achieve security.

This could be viewed as a natural pyramid based on the requirements of DNA – a survival equation approved and encouraged by DNA. It is essentially the free market system that those in the democratic societies live and work within. The heart of this system, or should I say the brain and controller of this system, could be the stock market, which can be shown to represent an almost exact analogue to the brain model I have described earlier. Figure 64 shows the layout and relationship of the constituent parts.

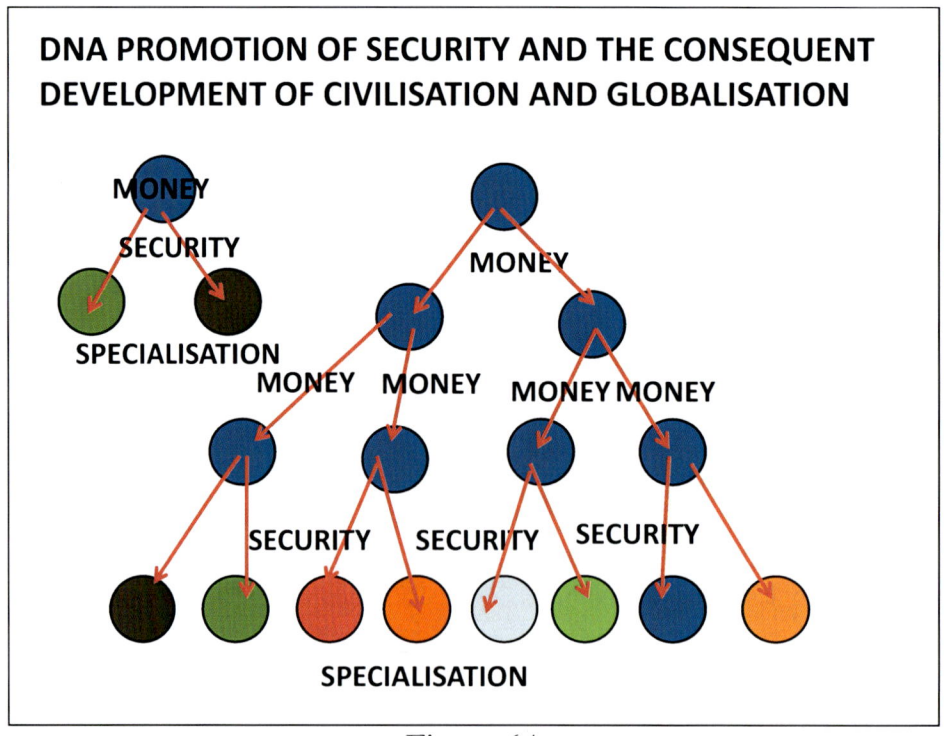

Figure 64

The stock market would then function as the processor, similar to the frontal lobe of the brain. It would be in essence the communal brain of all the contributing hosts (or investors). They receive information from the outside world about cooperative groups working to sustain and secure their DNA. The stock market (the communal frontal lobe) then assesses their enterprise and survival chances and gives them a survival score or share value for their stock. This is fed out to the DNA of the host contributors (shareholders) who wish to support this pyramid, which then feeds the frontal lobe with the 'dopamine-equivalent' money. This 'dopamine', or money, excites the cooperative groups with support and security to encourage the enterprise, which in turn will feed back to secure the host contributors. This way, provided the enterprise succeeds, the pyramid system sustains the contributing hosts and secures the DNA within us (Figure 65).

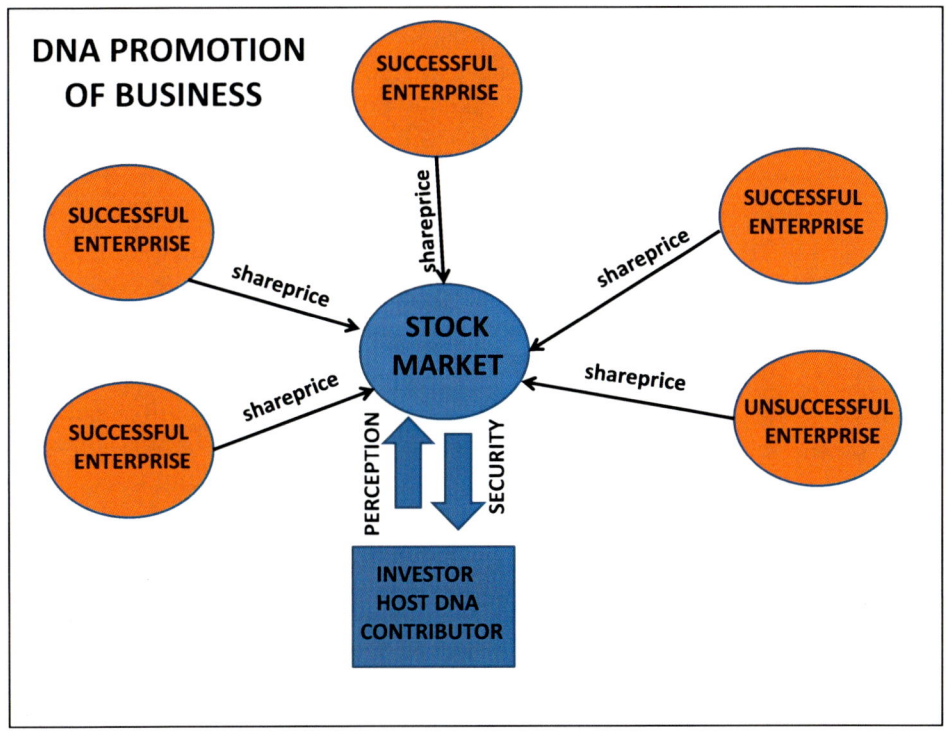

Figure 65

This could be viewed as a natural pyramid based on the requirements of DNA; a survival equation approved and encouraged by the DNA. It is possible to even transpose this view of the tripartite system from humans to the economy. We could imagine the stock market as acting similar to the frontal lobe of the brain. It receives current information, analyses it with respect to past information and gives a 'survival score' or share price to the stock. This condenses a lot of information regarding the health and stability of a business into a number. The share price is passed to the investors, who make decisions based on the likelihood of more profit being created by investing in that company. If they want to invest in it, they put in more money. This could be compared to the reptilian brain receiving the survival score and releasing dopamine into the body. If more money is put into a company, they can use that money to invest more and expand more. It encourages them to continue. If investors sell shares and the share price goes down, it is a sign there is a problem with the business, and it discourages that business model from being copied and continued.

The market economy pyramid may not be the only species of security pyramid favoured by DNA. Just as it evolved the variety of living species, DNA could have approved other species of security pyramids such as the early personal power pyramids and the more socialistic and communistic systems. It may well be that the survival advantages associated with the market economy are greater, especially within the context of a democratic society.

Both advances in technology and in language and communication have enabled us to speed up the evolutionary process through the ability to approve suitable new 'ideas' which aid survival. It could excite us to look for new and unexplored environments, both on Earth and in outer space. All this would increase the survival chances of life and promote its continuation within the Universe.

In the future, DNA may steer us towards building artificial life in the form of robots. At present, computers and computerised robots lack the essential ingredient of the survival process. Once humans can digitally simulate the 'tripartite system' within a robot armed with the essential appendages to replicate itself, the Universe will have a new self-sustaining life form. This life form would be capable of travelling and surviving the vast distances of space and inhabiting vast areas of the cosmos previously unavailable to humans. Such a life form would carry, in effect, a code comparable to the genetic code and, as a consequence, possess the same selfish drives as ourselves. However, this kind of development would come with a warning. Robots of this kind would now exist in competition with ourselves and represent a natural threat to our survival.

19

A PLACE FOR GOD

DNA = GOD

Figure 66

How would God and religion fit within a *Universal Life Force* driven by DNA?

Now, although I had surmised all of these hypotheses in a relatively cold, methodical and scientific manner, a comparison between God and DNA displays some uncanny similarities. For example, they both relate to one truth. In the case of Christianity, it is to serve the Lord and God (Figure 66). In the scientific hypothesis, we also have the one truth: to serve DNA. They both require a moral code of conduct and behaviour. They both adhere to the biological requirements for healthy reproduction of the offspring and for its care and security afterwards. They both see the need for a healthy social respect and benevolent co-existence with our neighbours.

One of the big stumbling blocks in religious ideology that prevents us from fully accepting its doctrines has been to explain the so-called presence of a God that can exist everywhere at the same time, be within you and without you at all times, in all living things, that is aware of our actions at all times, aware of our pain and suffering as well as our joy. A God that is all-powerful but at the same time needs our allegiance and prayers and demands our unquestioning loyalty. The questions and explanations have occupied theologians for centuries.

Why does a God who is all-powerful still require the allegiance of each individual on this planet?

How can this God allow so much indiscriminate suffering?

Why doesn't this God, who can be everywhere at once, show him- or herself?

In our present, more science-orientated world, it is difficult to deal seriously with these discussions. There is nothing tangible other than an ancient book to clarify our doubts or verify our explanations and belief in a God. We have to accept religion and all its fantastic stories on faith with the slim promise that obedience to the rules of this faith will eventually provide us with eternal salvation and a life ever after. As much as we all would want to have a benevolent, omnipotent God looking after all our interests, our present understanding of the world, and the Universe it occupies, does not correspond easily with such tenuous ideas.

Having said this, and as strange and superbly ironic as it may seem, DNA can be shown to, in fact, fulfil all these criteria just described. For example,

It exists within all our cells.

It knows what we are doing at all times.

It is aware of our pain and suffering as well as our joy.

It requires the allegiance of the host and consequently demands the host's unquestioning loyalty.

It requires the host to behave correctly to survive.

In effect, the behaviour demanded by DNA adheres to most biblical requirements.

DNA could be considered all-powerful and may exist, just like our more religious God in more powerful forms somewhere else in the cosmos.

All these points I have demonstrated in the earlier sections of this book. They are scientifically observable features, and the criteria can be examined and tested. The evidence is all around us.

Previously we have never been able to comprehend the existence of such a God before. But perhaps we can now although not in the literal form of a single omnipotent being. Nevertheless, it is an all-powerful, totally controlling force that requires our allegiance. It explains the almost supernatural qualities that a God would need to possess, such as being everywhere at one time, and at the same time, it explains the anomalous features we have wrestled with, such as the absence of true justice, that he doesn't come and show himself and interfere with the process, that he allows indiscriminate suffering, and so on. All people can gain comfort from feeling there is a higher authority watching over us. As just described, it is only natural that we should have an inherent feeling that we are part of something larger and that there is a higher purpose to our lives. However, in reality, it could be DNA that simulates this feeling and the inner sensation of a God within us.

Personally, I can live better with the idea that DNA arrived on this planet randomly as a survivor of some distant stellar explosion and that life simply began again. It does no harm to gain comfort in the idea that there are other imagined gods so long as the idea remains benign.

The problem, however, is that these thoughts tend not to remain private.

An individual with these beliefs seeks the comfort and additional security of other like-minded companions. They extend themselves into their own self-sustaining religious pyramid with an inbuilt power structure, which, in order to sustain itself, seeks to grow. As a result, there is a need to persuade and coerce others into the same beliefs.

There are many such pyramids attached to a variety of different religions. The consequent competition increases the thirst for more security, as do the demands of the inherent echelons of power within the ever-growing pyramid. Although the original concept may have been benign and comforting, the requirement to sustain this structure always leads to opportunism by individuals seeking to increase their security at the expense of others. The inevitable corruption destroys the security and comfort religion is supposed to provide. The threatened pyramid of power then relies on the enforcement of the concept, leading to the struggles we see in religions today. Political parties can seek to enhance the strength of their own power pyramid by linking themselves to a particular successful religious structure when it seems appropriate. This has been a ploy by governments throughout history.

Buddhism and Confucianism are notable religions that seem to be closer to the Universal Life Force tenets than other monotheistic religions. Buddhists seek no god and aim to reach a state of nirvana, being "at one" with the universe, following the path of the Buddha, Siddhartha Gautama, who went on a quest for Enlightenment around the sixth century BC. Some Buddhists believe all life is sacred and carry brushes in front of them to sweep away insects and avoid the destruction of any life. There is no belief in a personal god. Similarly the followers of Confucianism look for human heartedness, goodness, benevolence, man-to-man-ness, what makes man distinctively human and that which gives human beings their humanity. Both of these beliefs conform to the behavioural and survival requirements of the DNA.

In a way, the story I am presenting in this book is a form of religion. It relies on you believing the DNA story, just like Christianity relies on a belief that Christ was the Son of God. The fundamental difference is that the DNA story can be tested by all logical and scientific philosophy. It is supported by all we know about the human condition. In contrast, most religions rely on historical events that may or may not have occurred, which cannot be tested or rely on a narrow premise or personal testimony of an individual that lived more than 2,000 years ago.

The present explanation of the *Universal Life Force* being controlled by DNA meets all present scientific criteria and can stand up to modern-day philosophical scrutiny. It can be applied to all forms of life, whether plant or animal (or human). It is universal. As such, it offers a superior understanding of the human condition and a replacement for all other religious beliefs. It is not a formula for anarchy. It provides a total comprehensive solution which is rational and peaceful, demanding the cooperation and support for all that is living and without compromising the personal happiness and quality of life of any individual.

20

SAVE THE WORLD

If one was to accommodate the principles outlined in this hypothesis, would it change your life? The answer would probably have to be 'no'. This is because our behaviour is already a product of the DNA. What it does provide is a mechanism to understand our behaviour. It is always useful to be aware of why you do something or why you feel a particular emotion. It gives us more control of our lives. This way perhaps we can avoid some of the emotional pitfalls awaiting us. By consciously steering ourselves along the direction demanded by our particular DNA, maybe we could avoid unnecessary pain for ourselves whilst avoiding the anguish of others.

If future generations could be educated with these principles, and that everyone clearly understood them, perhaps it could result in a more stable society. And because the principles are universal, it could considerably improve the quality of life throughout the world.

An obvious first stage would be to understand that our ultimate purpose in life is to achieve security for ourselves and our offspring. It is vital to comprehend that we are all in competition but yet require the benign cooperation and support of everything around us to achieve security, happiness and contentment. Also that every individual requires their own unique blend of security and partner because the brain is an organic machine and the link between the intellectual processes (intelligence) and the ultimate DNA approval could vary enormously. We are all wired differently and would consequently achieve our security in a variety of ways. We need to perceive that at all times it requires the assistance and compliance of others, that assistance can come directly or indirectly via a multitude of complex relationships between men and women and the surrounding environment, that compliance means the benign support of the community and that means, in today's world, the world community. Our security can be threatened by the most remote peoples on the opposite side of the planet. The DNA philosophy demands the widest compliance for security and true contentment.

Most importantly, we need to appreciate **we have our own inner policeman** and as such would attempt to maintain security for the individual and its surrounding environment by controlling the amount of pleasure we receive. DNA, via the tripartite system, knows when you deliberately steal, whether it be somebody else's pen or one thousand pounds, or you aggrieve another individual by deliberately reducing their happiness by your gain. It would make you feel unhappy whether you have been observed or not. That an actual policeman has not seen you commit this crime may suggest escape from punishment. In the traditional sense, this might be true. However, DNA, via the tripartite system, would judge your act as you mull over the consequences. The threat of potential exposure and the subsequent wrath of society around you, or that of a particular individual, would constantly be reflected by restricting your opiate reward. Eventually this would gnaw at your ability to gain pleasure from the ill-gotten gains. In all cases when such actions are deliberate, we need to realise there would be a high emotional cost. In reality, police control would be unnecessary if people truly understood that such actions hold no long-term benefits for a life of contentment.

If everyone did understand the above principles and the personal consequences for them and their environment, I feel sure there could be benefits for everyone. Of course, I don't really expect to go out to impose these principles on the world; I merely consider the hypothesis. And of course, as with any hypothesis, there would be complications.

One of these is associated with the differences in culture and values people hold around the world. In some countries, for example, corruption is deeply ingrained in their way of life. It is in practice the people's way of creating their own welfare system. They grow up realising the only way of surviving the corruption from their own governments and the society around them is to do the same. It can be a vicious cycle of destruction that is almost impossible to break. Despite our best intentions, we have not, as yet, made any significant progress in assisting some of the world's most troubled societies. Aid agencies have put money into these countries attempting to improve their circumstances. Without proper management and support from the national, often corrupt, governments, these funds can sometimes fail to make any impact on the real problems.

The real problem may lie in the way the societies evolved. Many of them are still based essentially on the 'personal security (or power) pyramid' and sustain themselves via processes of force and coercion. Some cultures appear to have evolved a little further than the basic family unit and are thus constrained by the consequent limitations of such a system. Less corrupt societies (I say these words with a certain amount of scepticism) began in a similar manner but were able with time to escape some of the worst of this corruption (but not all) and develop a totally new security pyramid based on trade.

21

EVOLUTION OF A SECURITY PYRAMID

All societies began with the basic family unit. Such a unit was vulnerable, with only family members for protection. Grouping into larger associations, such as tribes, improved their chances of survival. Tribes provided security against attack and provided the material needs of food and building materials by sharing and shared labour. Gradually, and usually by force, tribes would be absorbed until ultimately forming kingdoms and eventually the nations we recognise today.

Societies based on the personal pyramid provided power for those who ruled and for those close to the rulers but not for all. With power came wealth and wives, all of which could provide an element of security for DNA. This was the 'personal security pyramid'. It was a brutal system which regularly cost innocent lives. It also required the coercion of usually unwilling participants to fight, something they would only do if the fear of non-cooperation was greater. Such life-threatening commitments sometimes offered the gain of being recognised as a brave fighting soldier, an accolade in earlier days which carried prestige and could attract female partners eager to gain the security of protection (the umbrella syndrome). The gain could also be expressed in terms of future security: 'We fight for our children so that they can live in peace'. In such statements, we can clearly hear DNA speaking.

The personal security pyramid always carried the continual threat of physical attack. Except for a few, there was consequently little security attached to such pyramids, especially for DNA. The earliest Greek societies with their associated Persian wars are typical examples. However, at the same time these struggles for power were ongoing, there was also another species of security pyramid growing within Greece based on the earliest attempts at democracy and trade. Here in Athens is evidence of a community employing rules designed and operated by the people to serve the people. This was clearly a system to be encouraged by DNA.

This was the dawning of 'democracy and fair trade'. Democracy and fair trade did not require physical power or even physical ability. Individuals could achieve security without force. Some individuals without any of these attributes could even become powerful and influential. In other words, the process could avoid physical conflict and the sacrifice of life, a feature far more attractive to DNA. All life is precious. DNA would thus steer us towards building this type of pyramidal structure. It allows for spontaneity and change and accommodates every kind of contribution both material and intellectual, features that are inherent in the *Life Force*. It is, in principle, the ultimate natural pyramid system and intrinsically linked to our internal, as well as external, requirements.

As explained earlier, it extends the fundamental security pyramid of the family forwards like an economic tidal wave and, as it does, incorporates all those involved. As the pyramid grows, all those involved have a natural interest in preserving the system to maintain their own security. So long as it is perceived to be the only realistic and practical way to obtain security, you would tend to immerse yourself deeper into the system. This has the consequent effect of pacifying all participants. They would not wish to rock the boat by inhibiting or destroying the system. There would be a natural will to preserve the status quo. This way, democracy and fair trade, despite the derisory press it can receive from cynics, and although not perfect, has an important potential peace-making role to play in the world. Everyone would be involved and reliant on the system to secure their future. The hope is no one would wish the system to fail and thus would try to preserve an environment of economic calm.

Unfortunately, there are still many ways to corrupt this idealised model. Fair trade very soon became free trade, which in the past amounted to raping underdeveloped nations of their raw materials. Some countries may allow fair trade, but others might put tariffs on their trades, which some argue is unfair gain. However, I would suggest tariffs are necessary for struggling economies. It enables their survival and thus their ability to compete and trade with larger economies. In addition, some countries quite simply wish to remain independent and in essence close their borders to the outside world.

Further complications can arise from individuals (e.g., dictators) who will try and combine both systems by using force to seize power over foreign but successful economies. Such a policy usually fails since they often do not appreciate the factors underlying that wealthy economy, the subtleties fuelling economic growth. Employing force to gain power over another nation is also a very expensive operation. In reality, it destroys the effective cooperation of the workforce previously responsible for the wealth of that nation. The cost of exploiting an antagonistic and defeated workforce is too high. Internal power struggles, and maintenance of the external boundaries to your newly acquired empire, all require constant attention and expense. The security gain for the DNA within this type of pyramid appears limited and offers little to the exploited majority. The benign nature of those involved cannot be guaranteed, and the chance of rebellion is consequently high. The eventual destruction of such a pyramid seems inevitable.

22

PEACE ON EARTH

Without the distortions just described, the underlying principle of 'democracy, enterprise and fair trade' could be viewed as an essentially peaceful system. There are losers in the process, but despite this negative aspect, survival may be still possible because of our social conscience and our ability to empathise and help those less fortunate. Essentially, the system is accessible to all, and in the present Western society, nearly all people are involved in some way. At the front end, anyone can start a business according to the skills he or she has to offer. At the rear, others may be employed to help sustain the growth of the business. Potentially, it can involve everyone, and thus, everyone is reliant on the continued success of the system.

The progressive spread of this system within the democratic nations of the world has done much to secure relations both within and between these nations. They are now intimately involved in each other's affairs and thus require the stability of these nations to continue and secure the survival of the particular businesses. Hopefully this will continue. The significance of national boundaries has decreased more and more in recent years. In my own particular discipline, a scientist living and working in Switzerland may actually be employed by a central office based in Norway, which is receiving work from a company in the USA, which has resources in West Africa and many other parts of the world. The security factor for DNA relies on the continued stability of this multidimensional, multinational business construction, which requires global stability. It requires the benign cooperation of all involved.

It could be envisaged that our future security pyramid would include the 'company' or 'skill' rather than the nation as its secure home. Your security pyramid or 'company' may not have a fixed or defined location since their function may well depend on a cooperation of individuals living and working from many world areas. National boundaries would have little significance. The most important centres would probably be the various stock exchanges located according to the focus of trade. International agreements with regard to law, employment, education, health and others already provide a wider sense of security. People would be free to locate according to their skills and their potential financial security. National origin, colour and culture now have much less significance. More important is the individual's skill and ability to form a successful business cooperation. However, I am well aware that human preferences are fickle, and any grand idea can fail because of the intransigence of individuals.

Commercial enterprise is often criticised for exploiting workers, especially during the formative years of the industrial and agricultural revolutions. Improved regulatory mechanisms and a realisation that improved conditions and a content workforce create more profit serve to reduce such problem areas. However, as the frontal wave of commercial enterprise travels through under-developed areas of the world, exploitation of cheap labour forces is still common, especially where corruption is endemic. Nevertheless, with time, gradual increases in wealth and standard of living could be achieved if the endemic corruption can be kept at bay. Hopefully, this can be improved if we are fully aware of what brings contentment, that is, we understand the controlling influence of the tripartite system and the genetic code of DNA.

If we accept the premise that globalisation of a security pyramid based on democracy, enterprise and fair trade could lead to world peace and harmony, what happens when all the underdeveloped areas of the world are developed and our natural resources spent? The lower-cost labour forces and our manufacturing ability will be lost. It would appear at first sight that the enterprise pyramid cannot continue to grow and be sustained. This conclusion would be true if the pyramid relied on the static premise of so-called cheap labour and natural resources. In reality, technology and world needs evolve and change, as do business structures. New business structures evolve and radiate outwards, just like new species, adapting to the new markets and resources. For example, the evolution in communications has allowed for a whole new range of businesses based on rapid networking around the world. Continued technological innovation and developments, driven by the DNA's requirement for security, could sustain the enterprise system indefinitely.

Nevertheless, there are still more uncertainties that can complicate peace and security. The most important is the mass migration of peoples from troubled and warring countries. It places immense stress on the neighbouring countries that receive them, especially when there are differences in culture and religion. There are no easy solutions to this.

Despite the positives outlined for the security pyramid described, I would like to point out a well-known drawback which brings it so much criticism. The drawback I refer to is 'greed'. Greed is the biggest threat to democracy, enterprise and fair trade. Most importantly, it affects our own personal contentment.

Greed by definition means too much, over-indulgence, indigestion. It is inextricably intertwined within the whole process. People confuse greed as being the vital motivator, the engine that drives the system onwards. In contradiction, I suspect it is not 'greed' that drives the engine but instead 'insecurity'. It is the requirement at all levels of the system to provide security for DNA. The company derives security from the input of money from the investor. The profits resulting from the growth of a company supplies the security for the investor. The problems arise when individuals can be observed to use the system to obtain more financial security than they could ever require. The sight of this imbalance obviously would incite discontent. It dismays the workers of the company who generally receive no direct benefit of these excesses, but more importantly, it angers the poorer areas of society. The system, despite its powerful nature, requires the compliance of all people to continue, and that includes the poor. Especially when they, through no fault of their own, cannot take part or benefit from these excesses. In such circumstances, the compliance of society in these areas cannot be guaranteed. Without the support of all involved, a corner of the democratic, enterprise and fair trade pyramid begins to falter.

So what causes greed, and can we control it? Again, perhaps with education about our DNA and its requirements, we could all be capable of understanding greed and the processes in our behaviour that could lead to it, but at the same time, the processes within our body that are already in place to control it.

We may be the host to DNA and as such have no choice but comply with its requirements. You must supply these requirements or else the DNA will not allow you to feel happy and content, and even then it would only allow you to feel content for brief moments and that these moments are tied only to the process of achieving security within the latter stages of resolving a survival equation. Only during the logical resolution stage of this equation, when the frontal part of the brain transfers its anticipation of being able to obtain security, would you be encouraged by the DNA with the release of dopamine. Only then would you experience pleasure. The final conclusion and solution only confirms the anticipated result and consequently receives little additional reward of pleasure. It is very important that we realise it is the 'anticipation' of a good result that gives us the feeling of pleasure and not the result. We do not receive a reward for receiving something that was already anticipated. This means, for example, that once we have anticipated that we will receive some money, we would not actually receive any more dopamine for the process of holding the money in your hands or putting it in the bank or just staring at it. The only way of deriving more pleasure out of this money is to 'think' of further equations that show additional security than previously envisaged. I suspect very soon, however, money alone would provide no new pleasure. This is why it is the process of making money rather than the actual amount of money that provides the pleasure. After a certain point, the increasing amount of money in itself would offer nothing significant in terms of pleasure, no more reward than the process of completing clues in a crossword. What it would do is attract the disapproval and frustration of those who could not take part in or benefit from and feel they are being made poorer by the process. This would be a threatening situation, and they would respond accordingly as they did during the French Revolution. It is up to our elected politicians and their governments to constrain this type of greed by imposing the appropriate level of income taxes. This has been achieved in Scandinavian countries, and their societies have become renowned for their fairer and contented lifestyle.

The same principle probably applies to 'greed' in all its forms even on a much smaller scale. In reality, even with the aid of education, it appears greed is unlikely to be controlled that easily. Greed is dangerous. It creates envy and possibly anger and violent retribution. If left unchecked, such retribution will lead to the eventual, if not sudden, destruction of the pyramid. History has shown this. More likely, however, is the realisation that there is more 'security' to be gained from controlling greed, just as there came the realisation that more 'profit', and as a consequence 'security', was to be gained from looking after the labour force than the former medieval system of exploitation. Only history will tell.

23

SURVIVAL OF THE CONTENTED

During the course of this short book, we have travelled through space and time to find the meaning of life. We have experienced all the early physical and chemical processes involved in the birth of the Universe, our planetary systems and finally life itself. I have presented thoughts which are highly individual and personal, perhaps controversial. To some, such thoughts may read as total fiction.

The story presented here, however, represents a new and unique model of our existence and a revolutionary perception of life and the Universe as we know it. It started as a simple quest to find happiness, about what controlled it and why it cannot be sustained. Along the way, I was obliged to visit several scientific disciplines. Although I was still only a young man, I could, by way of common sense, concentrated thought processes and deduction, arrive at conclusions that were rather startling.

A model emerged reasonably based on a sound understanding of all modern day scientific principles. It portrays our origins to be a part of a wider cosmic force. A *Universal Force* that possibly began billions of years ago in another stellar system, before our planet Earth ever existed.

I had discovered the process that drives physical processes and life to evolve and eventually develop such sophisticated structures as the brain and how the function of the brain could be fully explained by employing a tripartite concept, which is able to provide the mechanisms controlling our feelings, emotions, behaviour, morality (our inner policeman), and personality characteristics. I had also discovered the possible variations within the structure of the brain that may account for individual differences in our behaviour. Why some of us might be 'cool dudes' and others mere 'wimps'.

However, throughout all this, there had been one simple theme, one simple condition that appears to be controlling this *force*, from the beginning of time to the present day, and that is the 'conservation of energy'. This simple condition helps preserve the life of the Universe and ourselves.

From the explosive instance of the Big Bang, which released a colossal wave of energy from the grip of gravity, there has been a *forced* requirement to 'satisfy' the physical-chemical imbalances created within the evolving space it generates, that is, the Universe. A Universe required by the laws of mass and energy to correctly balance itself according to the requirements of its adjacent and neighbouring universes. By conserving energy within the basic matter that we are made up of and surrounds us, our Universe has managed to slow down the rapidly dissipating energy of space and its eventual extinction. It appears that by 'satisfying' the physical *forces*, it is able to sustain our current existence. Life, the biomass, assists the Universe in this balancing act. The fact that the life form of the human being is aware and able to think is purely incidental. We are here for a purpose: to help sustain the Universe. All our drive and willpower, our L*ife Force* (driven by the *Universal Force*) within, are directed towards this purpose so long as the Universe survives. Mankind has been searching for the 'truth' since the age of reason and consciousness began. Perhaps this is it.

Yet despite this bleak portrayal of our existence, we, as the host (possibly to a parasitic like organism), enjoy a unique and privileged position. The requirement of DNA to control its host, to steer and manipulate the host's behaviour to ensure survival, has at the same time (via the tripartite system), and by the input and restriction of opiates, provided an ability for the host to consciously feel and experience pleasure and pain. As a result, we are able to enjoy a vast array of emotional responses, including our elusive happiness, but also remorse, as the decisions we make affect our ability to survive and the security of the controlling DNA. Consequently survival situations offering security and a safe haven can provide the host with a 'feeling' of happiness and deep contentment. Similarly, when surrounded by children and a loving partner within this safe environment, the host can experience an even greater sense of fulfilment and joy. In addition, our senses can aspire to amazing moments of sheer ecstasy from the simulation of abstract survival scenarios created from the sonic attributes of sound (music), the visual simulations of light and shade (art), the simulated reality of stories and the security of winning (games). Provided the host behaves correctly with regard to the survival requirements of its controlling DNA, we, the host, can enjoy a life with an abundance of happy and contented moments – and just like when we were children, and placed in a playpen, the choice to behave is ours.

Despite the harsh nature of the above conclusions, there is one important note that gives this story a more optimistic ending. Our allegiance to DNA explains why some of us sense there is a God, in that all the conditions imposed on us as a host display uncanny similarities with religious doctrines. It is only natural that we should have an inherent feeling that we are a part of something larger and that there is a higher purpose to our lives. However, in reality it is DNA that simulates this inner sensation of God within us. Nevertheless, this sensation can still provide us with an added sense of security and calm.

In conclusion, the most important thing I would hope the reader might understand after reading this book is that the physics of our reality has led to an arrangement, a *force,* whereby the Universe is able to conserve energy and so effectively delay entropy and its subsequent disappearance. Life, as wonderful as it may seem, is merely a fortuitous development within this energy system. Human emotions, human existence and the meaning of life can all be understood from that base. If we understand the physics of why we feel happiness and pain, then we can better understand and manage our lives and emotions. In addition, we are now able to understand our desperate need to survive; to identify both the positive and negative effects of our selfish desire for contentment. Desires imposed and controlled by the genetic code of our DNA. In short, now we know the rules of the game, follow them and enjoy the pleasure they can give. Life will endure. We are all an integral part of the *Universal Life Force.*

REFERENCES

Campbell, J. 2009. *Margaret Thatcher*. Vintage Books London.

Egel, R., Lankenau, D.H. and Mulkidjanian, A.Y. 2006. *Origins of life: The primal self-organization* (includes Martin and Koonin, 2006; Forterre, 2006a; and Prangishvili, 2006).

Freud, S. 1923. *The ego and the id*. Internationer Psycho-analyischer.

Levy, M. and Miller, S.L. 1998. *Proceedings of National Academy*.

Lewisohn, M. 1986. *The Beatles live*.

Lewisohn, M. 1987. *In my life: John Lennon remembered*.

Lovell, P.V. et al. 2015. Living without DAT: Loss and compensation of the dopamine transporter gene in sauropsids (birds and reptiles). *Scientific Reports*. **5**(article number 14093).

Novacek, M. 2001. *The rise of mammals*. Evolution Library.

Douglas Adams, *The hitchhiker's guide to the galaxy*. 1978 BBC Radio 4.

ATTRIBUTES

Figure 1 modified from R. L. Atkinson et al. (1987, p.415).
Figure 3 from shutterstock..
Figure 24a modified from R. L. Atkinson et al. (1987, pp.60–62)
Figure 24c modifed from cs.boisestate.edu/"amit/teaching/342/lab/structure
Figure 25 from emaze.com.
Figure 28 The limbic system from stokeeducation.info.
Figure 29 The cerebral cortex from thearchivast.com.
Figure 30 modified from R. L. Atkinson et al. (1987, p.166).
Figure 32 modified from R. L. Atkinson et al. (1987, p.655).
Figure 33 Figure 34 modified from R. L. Atkinson et al. (1987, pp.158, 172).
Figure 35 modified from R. L. Atkinson et al. (1987, p.221).
Figure 37 from wondermondo.com.
Figure 38 from wikihow.com.
Figure 39 from connectedcoaches.org.
Figure 41 from kloiding.date.
Figure 42 from wordpress.com.
Figure 43 from wordpress.com.
Figure 44 from thedailymail.co.uk, eastlondonadvertiser.co.uk.
Figure 47 from dpchallenge.com.
Figure 49 from quora.com and paulontherun.
Figure 50 from discogs.com, exploringyourmind.com.
Figure 51 from metro.co.uk.
Figure 54 from dreamtime.com.
Figure 55 from her.ie.
Figure 56 modified from R. L. Atkinson et al., (1987).
Figure 57 modified from R. L. Atkinson et al. (1987, pp. 604, 216).
Figure 58 modified from R. L. Atkinson et al. (1987, p. 477).
Figure 59 from time.com.
Figure 60 from latimes.com.
Figure 61 from bbc.co.uk.
Figure 66 from en.wikipedia.org.

OTHER PUBLICATIONS BY THE AUTHOR

Cannon, S.J.C., Giles, M.R., Whitaker, M.F., Please, P.M., and Martin, S.V. 1992. A regional re-assessment of the Brent Group, UK Sector, North Sea. From Morton, A.C., Hazeldine, R.S., Giles, M.R., and Brown, S. Eds. 1992. *Geology of the Brent Group*. Geological Society Special Publication. 61.

Cole, J.M., Whitaker, M.F. and Kirk, M. 2016. Westphalian sequence stratigraphical cycles in the Southern North Sea and their hydrocarbon potential. From Riley, M. and Marshall, J., *Conference on Stratigraphical Advances in the Offshore Devonian and Carboniferous rocks*. UKCS and Adjacent Offshore Areas. Geological Society Special Publication.

Spencer, P.A., Whitaker, M.F., Dexter, J., and Vendeville, B. 1998. Dynamic sequence stratigraphic prediction and thin skinned extension: Examples from the Varg Trend, Norwegian North Sea. Abstract.

Siggerud, E.I.H., Whitaker M.F., Dexter, J., Spencer, P.A. 1999. Ichnofabric stacking significance for stratigraphic correlation within highly bioturbated marine siliciclastics: Case study from the Varg Field, Southern Viking Graben, Norwegian Sector. Abstract.

Thomas, B.M., Whitaker, M.F., Moller-Pedersen, P., Shaw, N.D. Hydrocarbon habitat of the Norwegian North Sea. Vol 1V Round Application Document.

Whitaker, M.F. 2017. Life and the Selfish Universe in *52 Things You Should Know About Palaeontology*. Palaeontology Agile Libre. Edited by Alex Cullum and Allard W Martinius pp.72-73.

Whitaker, M.F. 1984. The usage of palynostratigraphy and palynofacies in definition of troll field geology. In: *Sixth Offshore Northern Seas Conference and Exhibition 1984*, paper G6.

Whitaker M.F., Giles, M.R. and Cannon, S.J.C. 1992. *Palynological Review of the Brent Group*. Special Publications. 61. Geological Society, London.

Whitaker M.F. and Butterworth, M.A. 1978. Palynology of Carboniferous strata from the Ballycastle area. *Palynology.* 2, pp.147–157.

Whitaker, M.F. and Butterworth, M.A. 1978. Palynology of Arnsbergian strata in County Lietrim, Ireland. *Journal of Earth Sciences, R Dublin Society.* 1, pp.163–171.

SYNOPSIS

This story provides a scientific basis to understand behaviour, the complexities of emotions, the way we must live to achieve a satisfying life, our role within the vast Universe. It explains the *Universal Force,* the driver of the *Life Force* we feel within us and how these *forces* obligate and drive our selfish approach to life and survival. It explains the total dominance of DNA in our lives and how we appear to be subservient to its requirements. It places ourselves and all life within the physical systems of the Universe. It also explains how the Universe may function and our role in this process.

OUR PLACE IN THE UNIVERSE
-In reality, we are only a particular combination of chemicals conforming to, and driven by, the **Universal Force** to satisfy the physical laws of the cosmos.
-We carry out our lives, driven by the **Life Force,** the chemical balance of energy within DNA, in a blind determination to keep these laws, never fully realising the purpose of our actions.
-Our consciousness, our appreciation of form, beauty and everything else life has to offer, is just a 'tool' to aid our survival and the survival of the Universe.
-Basic particles, atoms, molecules, and others are all part of the process, representing different management situations of a dissipating energy resource as space expands.
-Life, the biosphere, is one of these management structures. Our role is only possible because of DNA. It carries the code to build required energy-saving structures. This way, it performs our function of energy conservation.
-Our survival is only incidental to the 'grand plan'. DNA doesn't care what it builds so long as it survives to conserve and manage a portion of the Universe's energy resource and passes on code for future generations to continue.
-What advantage is offered other than delaying the inevitable entropy? Entropy will prevail – or will it?
-The answer lies within relationships with parallel universes. Our Universe may exist in a relationship with other adjacent and parallel universes in the same way that atoms co-exist side-by-side with other atoms, merely a

continuation but a higher order of same physical principles. Atoms maintain internal integrity by close management of internal energy resources. In a similar manner, so could our Universe.

-The sequence of energy templates within our Universe implies a predictable evolution of energy management within a Universe. It may be true for adjacent universes. It follows that, for a universe to exist adjacent to other parallel universes, it would require carefully managed energy resources and bonding mechanisms. Perhaps stellar explosions, black hole development, anti-matter formation might create energy imbalances and facilitate required energy exchanges among adjacent universe systems.

NEW PRINCIPLES

-Pre-occupation of the Universe with energy management and conservation to prevent immediate decay or 'flash of light' syndrome.

-Orderly development of the Universe and its energy resources from the Big Bang controlled by 'harmonic resonance' to slow the rate of dissipation.

ENERGY TEMPLATES

-Energy templates manage energy dissipation and carve out defined benchmarks of energy conservation levels.

-It creates a ***force*** that requires the conservation of energy and inhibits entropy.

-DNA represents a lower energy template and the important mechanism of lower energy conservation with a unique ability to postpone and delay entropy.

-Survival of DNA (and its life forms) is essential in the orderly management process of the Universe. The DNA inherits the ***force*** which now becomes the **Life Force**.

THE TRIPARTITE SYSTEM

-This refers to the DNA development of the 'tripartite process', the most advanced part of evolution towards survival.

-All our thoughts, emotional experiences, behaviour can be steered by DNA and the tripartite process.

-It appears to control our most important personality traits, all our activities (personal, social and creative) to ensure a focus on survival.

-It steers us to exploit new environments.

ORIGINS

-The origin of DNA could be external and seeded from a previous stellar existence. DNA is a very efficient replicating machine, like an advanced virus, and can build its own host cells from available materials driven by the **Life Force** wherever it travels.

-It is the perfect mechanism to spread and ensure development of life throughout the Universe and time. Considered this way, the human being appears not to be an independent life form since its outer cellular content acts as a host for the inner RNA-DNA nucleus.

-The nucleus behaves like a parasitic virus. It appears to control all our bodily functions, carefully steering our behaviour towards survival via the tripartite system, which employs supply and restriction of drugs (natural opiates) to control our behaviour.

-We do this blindly, without knowledge of its existence. Our happiness depends on this.

A PLACE FOR GOD

-Results display uncanny similarities with religious doctrines.

-Both relate to one truth (religion – to serve our Lord and God; scientific hypothesis – to serve the DNA).

-Both require a moral code of conduct and behaviour.

-Both require healthy reproduction of offspring and its care and security afterwards.

-Both see the need for social respect and benevolent co-existence.

-Stumbling blocks in religious ideology to explain the presence of a God that can exist everywhere at the same time, be within you and without you at all times, in all living things, that is aware of our activities at all times, aware of our pain and suffering as well as our joy. A God all-powerful but needs our allegiance.

-Why does a God who is all-powerful still require allegiance of a single individual? How can God allow indiscriminate suffering? Why doesn't God show himself (or herself)?

-DNA can be shown to fulfil all criteria just described.

-For example, it exists within all our cells; it knows what we are doing at all times.

-It is aware of our pain and suffering as well as our joy.

-It requires the allegiance of the host and consequently demands the host's unquestioning loyalty.

-DNA is all-powerful and may exist just like our more religious God in more powerful forms somewhere else in the Cosmos.

-It is DNA that simulates the inner sensation of God within us.

CONCLUSION

For whatever reason, the principle appears to be that the Universe is preoccupied with energy management, and we are very important to the management of the lower part of the energy spectrum.

-So if anyone asks you 'Who are you and why are you here?', perhaps the answer should be 'I am driven by the Universal Life Force, and I'm here to conserve energy and help save the Universe'.

ABOUT THE AUTHOR

EDUCATION
BSc hons Geology (with Biology), London University
MSc Palynology, Sheffield University
PhD Palynology, Aston University, Birmingham

EMPLOYMENT
Geologist, NCB Opencast
Biostratigrapher-Geologist, SHELL UK
Biostratigrapher-Geologist, NORSKE SHELL
Chief Palynologist, SHELL INTERNATIONAL
Manager of Stratigraphy, GEOCHEM
Biostratigrapher-Geologist, SAGA PETROLEUM- NORSK HYDRO
Geologist/Stratigrapher, DET NORSKE PETROLEUM-AKER/BP

Manufactured by Amazon.ca
Acheson, AB